Haunted Wilmington...
and the Cape Fear Coast

Haunted Wilmington...
and the Cape Fear Coast

Brooks Newton Preik

Banks Channel Books
Wilmington, North Carolina

To my husband, Al,
and to my children, Angela and Richard,
for all their love and encouragement
and
To the memory of my mother,
Ann Lou Knox Newton,
who was my inspiration.

Acknowledgements

As much as I have wanted to write this book, I know I could never have done so without the help and encouragement of many other people. I am forever grateful to those who are listed below, but also to the ones not listed by name who have been a part of making this book a reality.

My very special thanks go to Ellyn Bache and to the members of my Writers Group for their enthusiasm and support for this project and for all their technical help.

For research assistance, I wish to thank Beverly Tetterton and JoAnn Galloway. I have relied heavily on the materials and books they have helped me to find in the Local History Room at the New Hanover County Library. And to Dr. James Beeler and the Library of the Lower Cape Fear Historical Society. Also to Jonathan Noffke at the Bellamy Mansion; Leland Smith at the Fort Fisher Historic Site; Anna Malicka of The Lewis-Walpole Library in Farmington, CT; Catherine Stribling for information on her grandfather, Captain John Harper; and John Golden, Folksinger and Storyteller.

For sharing their stories in personal interviews, I am indebted to Louise Fox McDaniel (also a granddaughter of Capt. John Harper, and a great niece of Joseph Bensel), Chris Fonvielle, Tatum Robertson, Mimi Welborn, Stuart Arrington Callari, Jean Hansen, Hannah Block, Suzanne Smith, Orrell Jones, Joyce Cooper, and Mary Frances Gause Oppelt.

And most of all, I am grateful to my husband, Al Preik, for being there to help whenever I needed him.

IF GHOSTS SHOULD WALK IN WILMINGTON

If ghosts should walk in Wilmington,
     as very well they may,
A man might find the night here, more
     stirring than the day;
Might meet with good John Vassall
     upon an airoplane
Or tackle bloody Blackbeard and
     hang him o'er again.

And loitering here and yonder and
     jostling to and fro,
In every street and alley the sailor
     folk would go.
The blockade runner derelicts
     emerging from the sands,
Along the shores of Wrightsville Beach
     that Pilot Death commands.

And all would berth together
     upon that silent tide,
The Southern Cross, the Stars and Stripes
     should wave there side by side.
All colors, creeds and nations,
     in fashion old and new
If ghosts should walk in Wilmington,
     as very like they do!...

from the poem by
Dr. James Sprunt
author of *Chronicles of the Cape Fear River
1660-1916*
(reprinted with permission)

Table of Contents

Preface

Over the years, and most particularly since I began the research and the interviews for this collection of ghost stories, I have learned that I am not alone in my fascination for the mysterious and unexplainable. It is a fascination that began when I was still young enough to cuddle safely in my mother's warm, comforting lap as she spun the scary yarns which my brothers and I begged her to tell.

When I grew up in Southport, in the days before television, storytelling was an essential part of everyday life and one which everyone enjoyed. In my high school years, there were always beach parties at Big Hill, a huge sand dune on the southern end of Long Beach. Back then, there were no restrictions against campfires on the beach, so after eating our fill of hot dogs and toasted marshmallows, we'd sit around the fire telling ghost stories. The atmosphere was perfect, and it was there that I first heard the tale of Theodosia Burr.

Later, when I became an elementary school teacher, I delighted in watching the faces of my students as I told them many of the same stories in this book, on gray, gloomy days when we couldn't go outside for recess. Rainy days became their favorite days—times to look forward to—and with the first drop to hit the window pane, I'd hear, "Tell us a ghost story, please, please!"

For the past twenty years, I have been a real estate broker, and in that capacity, I have had an opportunity to introduce many out-of-state homebuyers to this community. My "newcomer tours" always begin with the historic down-town area, and once again, I am able to indulge my passion for telling local legends. Sometimes months, or even years, pass before I see some of these homebuyers again, yet they always seem to remember those ghostly introductions to Wilmington. The details of the sales contracts have long since faded from memory, but none of them have ever forgotten the story of Samuel Jocelyn, the man who was buried alive.

These tales of the supernatural are an intrinsic part of the rich folklore of the coastal area, and they have been written with as much attention to authenticity and historical accuracy as possible. Many people have asked, "Are these ghost stories true?" That, I cannot answer. I leave it up to you, dear reader; you must decide for yourself.

Brooks Newton Preik
Wilmington, NC
July 1995

Spirit From the Sea

Joan Kaiser

"O lost, and by the wind grieved,
ghost, come back again."
Thomas Wolfe
1900-1938

Spirit from the Sea

The storm which had raged all day was growing worse. Rain pelted the heavy wooden storm shutters, demanding entrance. Like eerie shrieks of a banshee, the relentless wind wailed, a portent of the death and destruction the Nor'easter would wreak before the coming of dawn. The proprietress of the Stuart House, an inn on the riverfront in Smithville, dozed fitfully. Mary Elizabeth Stuart had weathered brutal storms many times, but this one held a particular terror. Yesterday her son, Joseph Bensel, and four of his companions, all coastal pilots, had set out to sea in search of a passing ship that might need their skilled guidance through the treacherous waters of Cape Fear. Their pilot boat was an open sea dory, with four oars and a sail, the type most of the pilots used—sturdy, but no match for a storm such as this. Since the onset of the storm, she had waited for word of Joseph's return. None came. With a heavy heart, she prayed that his small boat would find shelter somewhere along the coast, but in truth, she imagined it being tossed about like a piece of driftwood in the angry sea.

1

The pilots, in their quest for ships, often had to travel as far north as Cape Lookout, some ninety nautical miles distant. It was 1872, almost a decade after the War Between the States. Times were hard, and rivalry for the piloting jobs was fierce. Mary Stuart's son, Joseph, had been able to keep his position at the forefront of the competition due to the skills and daring he had developed during the war. His reputation as the pilot of a successful blockade runner, the *City of Petersburg,* was widely known. On sixteen runs he had dodged the Yankee gunships, navigating the coastal waters and the Cape Fear River as deftly and stealthily as a crocodile stalking its prey.

Oddly, it was the memory of the dangerous days of the war that gave Mary Stuart some small comfort now. She knew that if anyone could ride out a storm in safety, Joseph could. Yet, even though her daughter, Kate, and the few guests who remained had retired hours before, Mary Stuart could not bring herself to go upstairs to bed. Instead, she lay down on the daybed in the living room. Unable to shake the feeling of foreboding that had been with her all day, she tossed and turned, alert to every change in the storm's assault.

The wind stopped abruptly and in the sudden silence, a well-known sound, the loud click of the gate latch outside, caused Mary Stuart's heart to race in hopeful anticipation. There were footsteps on the porch. She could not see the clock, but she knew that midnight had long since passed. She had checked the time just a short while earlier when she had gotten up to stoke the fire. The flames still danced brightly in the fireplace.

The footsteps grew louder, nearing the door, then

stopped as someone struggled to open the heavy portal secured tightly against the malevolent wind. It's Joseph, she thought with great relief, for who else would come to her door at this late hour on such a night. Miraculously, he must have brought his boat to a sheltered mooring at the dock next door. He was stopping by her house to calm her fears about his safety before going to his own home on the other side of the village. He always did.

The door opened. A man entered the room, wet and dripping in heavy rain gear. Shutting the door behind him, he turned toward the warmth of the fireplace. Mary Stuart was overjoyed to see her son.

She sat up and called out to him, thinking that he might not have seen her on the daybed in the near darkness.

"Joseph."

There was no answer. She rose, her joints stiff, unaccustomed to the hardness of the daybed. She walked toward him, happy to see him unhurt, yet puzzled that he had made no reply.

She saw the familiar figure clearly outlined in the firelight. Placing his hands on the mantel, Joseph leaned forward and spit into the fire. As the tobacco juice hit the flame, she heard it sizzle. It was a sound she knew well, from a habit long associated with her son. Years later, she would still remember that distinctive sizzle each time she told the story of that night.

"Joseph," she called again.

Again, there was only silence.

A low rocking chair stood just in front of the hearth. She watched as her son sat down, his back to her, with his shoulders hunched forward in a posture of extreme weariness. Perhaps he is too exhausted to speak, she thought— a feeling she could well understand. Approaching the chair, she called his name a third time and reached out to place both hands in a gesture of comforting love upon her son's shoulders.

Happiness at his return instantly turned to horror!

Her outstretched hands hung suspended in space. The rocking chair, now vacant, ceased its motion. The son she had seen—had even heard spit into the fireplace—had vanished. She was alone in the room.

Dawn came. The deadly storm was over. Early in the day, a messenger brought the tragic tidings Mary Stuart had been expecting. Joseph Bensel's boat, *The Mystery*, torn apart by mountainous waves in the midst of the Nor'easter's fury, was lost without a trace. There were no survivors. Only one body was ever recovered.

*   *   *

Joseph Bensel was not forgotten. In the old cemetery in Southport, (formerly Smithville), there is an aged stone obelisk that rises high above the other monuments. It was erected in 1879 as a lasting memorial to the bravery of the five pilots lost in the Northeaster of 1872 and to five more who perished in the hurricane of 1877 aboard the *Mary K. Sprunt*. Carved there, along with the names of the drowned seamen, is this fitting and poignant epitaph:

> *"The winds and the sea sing their requiem,*
> *and shall forevermore."*

The pilot, Joseph Bensel, was my great-grandfather.

A
Voice from the Grave

Davis Canady

*"The boundaries which divide Life from Death
are at best shadowy and vague.
Who shall say where the one ends,
and where the other begins?"*

Edgar Allan Poe
1809-1849

A Voice From The Grave

Though the heat of the summer night was unbearable, heavy draperies were pulled tightly over the open windows shutting out any breath of air that might be stirring. Gloom blanketed the room like the black velvet folds of a burial pall. A single candle burned without flickering in the oppressive stillness. Alexander Hostler sat as he had for two days and nights, in an almost catatonic state, devastated by the untimely death of his best friend. Hostler's face was a mask of agony. The silence in the room was broken only by the rhythmic ticking of a mantel clock... until a voice called his name.

"Alexander"

He whirled around, angry at this intrusion into his private moments of grief.

He was ill prepared for what he saw. The warm blood that had signaled his anger seconds before now felt like icewater in his veins. A phantom figure, seeming to glow from its own unearthly light, stood before him in the darkness. The ghostly countenance was that of his dead companion, Samuel Jocelyn.

Plaintively, the figure spoke—a hollow, far away sound—but nonetheless recognizable as the voice of his friend. It was not the sound, but the words themselves which filled him with unimaginable terror.

"Alexander, how could you let them bury me when I was not yet dead?"

In utter disbelief and panic, Alexander cried out, "It cannot be... surely not!"

"You have but to open my coffin to know the truth," the specter replied, and vanished.

Shock gave way to fear and then to doubt. Alexander tried to convince himself that what he had seen was a product of his imagination. In his distraught state he must be hallucinating, he reasoned. It could not be true! The idea of his friend being buried alive was inconceivable. He knew he must say nothing to anyone of the strange occurrence, lest they think him deranged from melancholia and depression. He decided to put the incident out of his mind.

But how could he put aside such a monstrous thing when the events of the past week and all the years before would not leave him in peace for a single instant? He was besieged by a million mental images of happier times, each taunting him with the grim reality of his loss.

Since early childhood the boys had been inseparable. Their Sunday school teacher even nicknamed them Jonathan and David because their devotion to each other so resembled that of the two young Biblical friends. As youngsters they had played along the riverbank, reliving the stories of pirates long dead and searching for buried treasure. They had fished there, learned to row a dinghy, done a thousand and one things that boys do. They had gone through school together, shared the same teachers, agonized over the mysteries of algebra and geometry. When the time came to court the young ladies, they were present at every Cotillion, learning the social graces that were expected of polite Southern gentlemen, always attracting the fairest in the crowd.

Samuel was the son of a prominent Wilmington attorney, and both he and his friend, Alexander Hostler, enjoyed a fine reputation in the community. Their circle of friends was wide. The two young men, in their early twenties, were known to be of impeccable character, with the highest moral standards. No hint of scandal had ever touched their lives; no major sadness or tragedy had occurred to mar their youthful happiness. No one had ever heard the two say a cross word to each other. Conjoined twins could not have been closer.

As they grew to manhood their childish games turned to more intellectual pursuits. They were fascinated with the study of metaphysics and often engaged in discussions with their friends about such matters. They were the favorites among their peers and much respected for their insights and observations concerning things philosophical and spiritual.

One warm summer day in the year 1810, in just such a discussion, the talk turned to life after death. Despite the friendly ridicule and teasing of many in the group, Alexander and Samuel stood firm in their conviction that communication beyond the grave was a possibility. They even made a pact that afternoon, witnessed by all: if one of them should die, he would try in some way to communicate with the living friend. Undaunted by the laughter of their comrades, the two men were convinced that some form of communication would indeed be achievable. Months later, those very skeptics would remember that conversation in detail.

Ironically, horseback riding, the sport which Samuel loved most and at which he excelled, was the only activity the two men did not enjoy in common. Perhaps Alexander was afraid of horses, or perhaps it bothered him that he was not as skillful a horseman as his friend. Whatever the reason, those times when Samuel went riding were the only times the two were not together.

Samuel loved nothing better than to race his horse along the low-lying sandy roads near the river. And it was there—under the sprawling branches of a giant live oak tree—that his almost lifeless body was discovered just a few months after the life and death pact had been made. Samuel was such an accomplished equestrian that Alexander could hardly believe the terrible accident had befallen him. Two men in a horse-drawn cart happened along the way shortly after Samuel Jocelyn was apparently thrown from his horse. He was lying unconscious beside the road. His horse was calmly grazing just a short distance away. As the men drew closer, they recognized Jocelyn and rushed to place his badly bruised body in the cart. They hastened to reach his home, uncertain whether Jocelyn was alive or dead.

His parents summoned the family doctor who came immediately and did all within his power to revive the young man, but a few hours later Samuel Jocelyn was pronounced dead without ever having regained consciousness. The body was prepared for burial and, according to custom, remained for viewing in the family home for two days before the funeral and interment in St. James Churchyard on the corner of 4th and Market Streets.

It would be impossible to describe the grief that Alexander Hostler felt at the death of his lifelong friend. No words of consolation could assuage his anguish and remorse. He blamed himself for not being there, thinking that in some way he might have prevented the terrible accident. Hostler's family and friends knew that he wished only to be left alone in his despair, and so he had been, until the voice of his dead friend disturbed his solitude.

The night following that first ghostly visitation, Alexander Hostler, lost once more in his doleful reverie, sat in his darkened room. As if by appointment, the voice of Samuel Jocelyn called his name and once again asked the terrifying question.

"Alexander, why did you let them bury me when I was not yet dead?" This time the tone was more insistent.

"But you *were* dead," Alexander cried in reply. "The doctor said you were, and I saw you myself." He began to sob uncontrollably.

"Within my coffin lies the truth. Look there and you will know." The spirit spoke and was gone.

Hostler was beside himself, yet he was even more convinced than on the previous night that what he had heard was impossible. He was certain that in his despair his imagination was playing cruel tricks with his mind. Again, he said nothing to anyone for fear of being thought mentally unstable.

The story might never have been told had it not been for a third and far more terrifying appearance by the apparition on the following night. This time the voice implored Alexander to validate its grisly revelation by examining the contents of the coffin.

Knowing now that there would be no rest for the spirit or himself if he did nothing, and convinced by this time that he was not hallucinating, Alexander contacted a good friend who was also a citizen of much prominence and credibility in the community. The man's name was Louis Toomer. Something in Hostler's manner must have persuaded Toomer that his story was true, for together the two went to the parents of Samuel Jocelyn with their awful tale. The Jocelyns gave their permission for the body to be disinterred, but they stipulated that the investigation must be done in secret so as not to attract curiosity seekers.

Accordingly, the plans were made, and the next night shortly after midnight Hostler and Louis Toomer made their way stealthily to the gravesite. The earth was still soft, easy to turn with their shovels, and in a very short time the coffin was exposed. Toomer held the carefully shielded lantern and the two men noted with horror that one side of the coffin had been loosened. Fearful of what he would find, Alexander anxiously pried open the lid. In the dim light, a gruesome scene was revealed.

The white satin lining of the casket was torn and bloody, the burial clothes lay in shreds. Most horrifying of all, the body was lying face down. Alexander Hostler sank to his knees, covered his eyes with his hands, and rocked back and forth in his wretchedness. His agonized cries of mourning split the silence of the night in a wild, primitive lament.

For the rest of his life, Alexander Hostler would live with the sorrow and pain of the hideous truth he had uncovered that night.

The Thespian Spirits of Thalian Hall

Jeffrey Hull

".... ghosts which everybody talks about
and few have seen."
La Rochefoucauld
1613-1680

The Thespian Spirits
of Thalian Hall

Not everyone believes in ghosts. But if you ask
Wilmington native, Chris Fonvielle, whether he believes, his
answer is a resounding, "Yes!" His experiences in Thalian
Hall leave no doubt. He knows he has seen them.

"I was sixteen at the time," Chris recalls, " but I
remember vividly what I saw that day. The physical and
emotional sensations I felt, even now, defy any verbal defini-
tion." It was late in the afternoon that spring of 1969, when
Chris and four of his classmates joined Tatum Robertson,
then president of the Thalian Association, for what they
termed a "Ghost Excursion." Taty, as she is fondly called,
was easily persuaded to take the boys on a tour of the old
theatre because of her fascination with the ghostly legends
and some of her own psychic experiences there.

"Bring flashlights," she told them, planning to keep
the atmosphere as spooky as possible.

Taty met the group at the stage door. She began by
giving them a brief history of the hall, explaining that many
believed it had been constructed over the site of an ancient

burial ground. As her low voice droned on, the boys strained to see into the balcony, hoping to catch a glimpse of the three phantom actors, dressed in Edwardian costume, who on many occasions had been observed there. Often, Taty told them, a member of the cast would be dispatched to go up and investigate, only to discover three turned-down seats, left that way, it seemed, in mocking testimony of their previous phantasmal occupants.

The anxious band of intrepid ghost hunters, reasonably satisfied that no one was observing them from the balcony, made their way carefully down the aisle to the back of the theatre. The boys elected not to use the flashlights. It was dark inside, but their eyes had adjusted, and enough light filtered through the cracks and under the doors to create an eeriness well suited to the occasion. They shivered nervously.

Passing through the gallery lined with yellowed photographs, signed by many of the actors who had graced the historic stage, Taty pointed out three in particular. By their costumes, she said, it had been determined that they were the actors who were thought to haunt the balcony area. The fading pictures heightened the boys' mood of expectancy, but alas, a tour of the two balconies proved uneventful and the group descended the stairs dejectedly.

The theatre was growing darker, and the five stalwarts, by now thoroughly disappointed, prepared to leave. As they stood in the foyer, straining to see the stage, they were unexpectedly startled by an uncanny presence sitting in one of the seats about sixty feet away to their right.

"The apparition had no distinct form—it was more of a glowing light—but it was definitely a presence that we could feel as well as see," Chris relates. There seemed to be an unusual suspension of time and a strong sense of something not of this world.

The boys were sure they had not seen the entity come in. They just knew that suddenly it was there—and just as suddenly, a few seconds later, it was gone.

Stunned, they made their way back to the stage. They fell breathlessly onto a sofa and some chairs that were part of the set for a recent play, momentarily unable to speak. Then, two of the boys, maybe in a show of bravado or perhaps to check one final time for the "turned-down seats," decided to return to the balcony.

When they did not come back right away, Taty grew anxious and thought it best to check on them. She left the stage, taking the identical route the boys had taken.

"Just as she made her turn to go up the middle aisle," Chris said, "I realized a man was sitting there in the darkened theatre. Again, I was not aware of when or how he arrived, but he was there, and just as she walked past him, the man stood up and followed Taty up the aisle. Sam and Tom, two of my friends, saw him too, but Taty seemed oblivious to his presence." Unlike the first apparition, this one had a definite form and a distinctive though transparent appearance.

"He wore a frock coat and knee boots in an Edwardian style and he was tall and slender," Chris said. The specter followed Taty all the way to the back of the auditorium. When she turned left to go up to the gallery, he turned right and both disappeared from sight. Soon Taty returned with the two boys, and the others clamored to reveal what they had seen.

Oddly, Taty was not surprised. It was not the first time such a figure had been seen, she said. Many had told of similar sightings. The description of the man was always the same.

* * *

By 1994, Tatum Robertson was long retired and in fragile health, but her memory of the years when she was involved with the Thalian Association remained clear and vivid. Her pleasure in those recollections was obvious during our interview, as she confirmed Chris's story and continued with more of her own.

Taty remembered one night when she and the late Hester Donnelly, a well known local artist, were painting frantically in an effort to finish some scenery for a dress rehearsal and opening night.

"We went to dress rehearsal and we just could not get the work done. We stayed till three o'clock in the morning, and finally, I told Hester we'd just have to leave and come back early in the morning."

Totally exhausted, the two locked up and left. No one else had a key to the building.

"When we went back at seven," Taty continued with a smile, "the 'flats' were finished. Compliments of the ghost!"

On another occasion, Taty was charged with assisting the leading lady in a three-minute costume change. The actress had only that much time to leave the stage, go downstairs to a dressing room, change, and return for the next scene. Each night the Victorian outfit with dozens of tiny buttons down the back had to be unbuttoned in advance.

"I told them to delay a minute and went tearing

downstairs to the dressing room in a panic. I found the dress, lying across a chair, ready as usual with all the buttons undone. Nobody else had been near that room."

Similar stories and other versions of the same stories have been told by countless numbers of people associated with the Thalians and the hall itself. During the fifties and sixties, several actors, deciding that the spirit-filled atmosphere of the theatre lent itself to such events, held a series of seances there. They failed to summon any spirits and eventually gave up.

Skeptics argue that the ghosts in the balcony were only illusions caused by the theatre lighting. They say there are equally plausible explanations for the other manifestations. Despite such attempts to explain away the phenomena, generations of local thespians agree: something enigmatic and supernatural has always been a part of Thalian Hall.

"The ghosts were friendly," Tatum Robertson said. "They did things to help us, and sometimes they just wanted to watch." Referring to the extensive renovations at Thalian Hall in recent years, she said, "It's all too modern now. I think the ghosts are gone."

With more than six hundred performances and activities taking place in the modernized facilities yearly, things are not as personal as they used to be. It is possible that the ghosts feel they are no longer needed and have left for other haunts.

Yet perhaps, late at night, when only the echoes of the past are left to fill the old theatre, they sit in the balcony still, watching phantom performances on stage.

Or maybe...just maybe, they are hiding in the wings, hoping to be summoned for one final curtain call.

Mystery at
Maco Station

Dan Welborn

"There is nothing impossible in the existence of the supernatural: its existence seems to me decidedly probable."

George Santayana
1863-1952

The Mystery Light of Maco Station

Today cars whiz past on a modern four-lane divided highway. The old wood-burning trains which used to rumble into Maco Station are no more. Even the tracks which lay rusting in the swampy woods have long since been removed. Though the decay of passing time and the Seaboard Coast Line have obliterated all physical evidence, the legend of the Maco Light and the headless ghost of old Joe Baldwin live on. Those who have seen the mysterious manifestation (and there are many) can never forget the awesome experience.

The story began in the late 1860s. Joe Baldwin was a conductor on one of the trains that regularly came through Maco Station, a point on the Atlantic Coast Line Railroad about fourteen miles west of Wilmington. One night as his train was nearing the station, Joe discovered to his horror that the rear coach on which he was riding had become uncoupled and was slowing to a stop on the tracks. Behind him, another train was fast approaching! In an effort to warn the oncoming train and avoid a terrible collision, Joe grabbed a signal lantern and began waving it frantically from the rear platform. Either the engineer of the second train did not see the desperate signaling, or he was heedless of the danger that lay ahead. Whatever the reason, the train continued on its collision course. It hurtled toward the disabled car at a terrific speed. It crashed into the stalled coach with a force that spread wreckage in every direction. Witnesses said that Joe Baldwin's lantern waved to the very end, then was seen careening through the swamp where, amazingly, it continued to give out a steady glow until it was retrieved. Rescuers digging through the carnage found a gruesome sight. The crushed, bleeding body of the brave conductor had been decapitated. Legend has it that his severed head was never found.

Not long afterwards, folks in the area began to report the sighting of an inexplicable light which seemed to come up out of the swamp and move slowly down the tracks. At times, the light seemed to hover about five feet above the tracks weaving back and forth like the swinging of a lantern. At other times, the light moved in an arc and disappeared into the swamp. One story from 1873 told of a second light that appeared to some of the railroadmen. This light came from the opposite direction, drawing closer and closer to the first one until they met. Strangely, an earthquake in 1886 caused the second light to disappear, and from that time on the Maco Light, as it came to be known, was a single light, thought by many to be the signal lantern that old Joe Baldwin waved about as he searched for his head.

The story received national attention in 1889. President Grover Cleveland aboard the presidential train stopped at Maco Station (or Farmer's Turnout as it was called in earlier years). The train, a wood-burner just like Joe Baldwin's, stopped to refuel and take on water. President Cleveland, possibly tired of being cooped up in the noisy, stuffy train, took the opportunity to get a bit of fresh air and proceeded to walk down the tracks. Upon seeing a brakeman with two signal lanterns, one red and one green, the President inquired as to why there were two lights instead of the customary single signal. The brakeman's reply elicited more questions from the President, and before Cleveland departed he had heard the tragic tale, including the fact that two lanterns were used at Maco Station so that they would not be confused by the train engineers with the ghost light of old Joe Baldwin.

Accordingly, the story reached Washington, D. C., and a short time later an investigator from that city visited Maco to search for the light and to try and find a scientific explanation for its occurrence. He saw the light but left town unsatisfied as to its source. He did determine, however, that the light was not the *ignis fatuus*, or will-o'-the-wisp, that is frequently associated with similar swampy locations.

Others have tried to solve the mystery of the light, but it has managed to defy all such attempts. Even a machine-gun detachment from Fort Bragg was once dispatched to the area. During their brief encampment, soldiers tried in vain to "capture" the light or at least to come up with an answer to the mystery of its appearance. They even used their weapons to shoot at the phenomenon. Alas, the mighty U.S. Army, unbeaten in two world wars, was helpless in the face of this "enemy" of unknown origin!

A scientific research team from the Smithsonian

Institute, a group of electronic engineers, and noted parapsy-chologists including the internationally known Dr. J. B. Rhine, one-time director of the now-defunct parapsychology laboratory at Duke University, all had a go at explaining the mystery. Their efforts met with the same results. Dr. Rhine and others thought perhaps it might be the reflection of automobile lights, but this explanation could not account for the fact that the light appeared long before the advent of the automobile.

From time to time over the years there has been a resurgence of interest in the Maco Light. *Life Magazine* included the legend in a feature article in December, 1957. About the same time, the "Allen Douglas Show" on station WKYC aired the story of the light, and the local public library received requests from all over the country for more information on the light.

The most widely publicized occasion happened in 1964 when a local organization hired the then-popular author and ghost hunter, Hans Holzer, to conduct an inves-tigation. Hopes ran high that finally the enigma would be solved. Holzer made a big production of his quest, received a tremendous amount of attention from the media, gave a lecture at Brogden Hall (and sold a significant number of autographed copies of his recently published book, *Ghost Hunters*), but he came no closer than anyone else to a plausi-ble solution. He included the story in a collection of strange tales that he subsequently wrote, entitled *Phantoms of Dixie*.

The local newspaper has published countless articles since the light first appeared, radio broadcasts have fright-ened listeners with the ghostly tale, television personalities have retold the story on Halloween specials, but perhaps the best description of the light appeared in an article in *The State* in July, 1934, written by Charles N. Allen. Anyone who has ever witnessed the light will feel a chill of remembrance.

" The eerie-looking thing sways a little and begins creeping up the tracks. Your eyes are magnetically glued to its movements.....The thing comes on..... It becomes brighter as its momentum increases... It glares at you for a moment like a fiery eye, as if jeering at your bewilderment, then it speeds rapidly back down the tracks as if hurrying away from some unseen danger."

Thousands of people through the years have seen the light. Some are more graphic in their descriptions than others, but the accounts are all basically the same. Mimi Welborn, a native of Wilmington, recalls visiting the site often when she was a teenager in the fifties. "We'd get a guy with a truck loaded with hay, and we would all pile in the back, drive out there and scare the living daylights out of ourselves. Sometimes we would have to wait, but sooner or later it would appear. If we walked toward it, it would back off, but if we just stayed still, it would come toward us. It was eerie. It had a sort of swinging motion. I get real nostalgic when I think about it. It was part of our history, and now it's gone."

Indeed, since the dismantling of the railroad tracks in 1977, the light seems to have vanished for good. Its disappearance after so many years of keeping its lonely vigil has occasioned much speculation. Some say it is because the tracks are gone, and the trains no longer stop at Maco Station. Others attribute the light's absence to the fact that the area is now built up, and with so much activity the atmospheric conditions conducive to its appearance have changed. But those who know the story or who have seen the famous light hope that the search is finally over and that old Joe Baldwin has at last found eternal rest.

The Return of
the Harpist

Elizabeth Picklesimer

*"A lively understandable spirit
Once entertained you.
It will come again."*
Theodore Roethke
1908-1963

The Return of the Harpist

The year was 1882. The place, a quaint fishing village that hugged the shoreline where the Cape Fear River ended its long journey to the Atlantic Ocean. Tales of men lost at sea were not unusual in this quiet town. Violent storms had taken the life of many a Smithville sailor through the years. But that particular August afternoon was warm and sunny with no hint of hazardous weather conditions, a perfect day for pleasure craft. No one could have anticipated the disaster which struck without warning.

*   *   *

Antonio Caseletta, a harpist, was an Italian immigrant who had arrived in Wilmington from New York with his wife, his young child, and two other musicians. Some said the three men were brothers, but no one is sure. The musicians, tired of the miserable, unbearable cold of New York, had booked passage on a steamer and headed as far South as their limited funds would take them. Happy to be in a climate that more nearly resembled the temperate climes of their native Italy, the men, though penniless, were optimistic. They hoped to find work as street musicians, but, unlike New York, Wilmington was not a city that lent itself to such entertainment. There was even a city ordinance prohibiting it. Try as they might, they could not get a job.

They had almost given up hope when Captain John Harper, master of the steamboat *Passport* (a forerunner of his famous ship, the steamer *Wilmington*), heard of their plight. Captain Harper loved music, and there was something about these poor down-and-out musicians that touched him. He told them about the Hotel Brunswick, a large sprawling inn on the waterfront in Smithville, and urged them to seek employment there. He even made arrangements for them to accompany him at no charge on his daily round trip to Smithville. Not only was the hotel a popular place for summer guests, dances were held there almost every night. Captain Harper assured them they would find employment there and promised them an introduction.

The Hotel Brunswick had originally been a private residence, and unlike other Smithville homes it boasted a deep basement constructed with ballast stones from cargo ships. The basement was used as a tavern with entrances under either end of a huge front porch that extended the length of the house. There was some evidence that old tunnels ran beneath the house, and rumors held that the tunnels had been used by pirates during the time when the buccaneers pillaged the North Carolina coast. There were even reports in later years that "pieces of eight" were found on the grounds.

In the early 1880s, a prominent physician, Dr. Walter Curtis, became the proprietor, and expanded the structure to cover almost the entire block. With its beautiful views of the harbor, it soon became a mecca for merchants and summer tourists. Rates were as low as $5.00 per month for long-term guests. Nightly dances in the ballroom were a drawing card for the hotel and were often followed by moonlight cruises. It was the ideal place for the three young musicians, and as Captain Harper predicted, they were hired.

Things went well for the musicians. They were popular with the guests and the townsfolk alike. Their position seemed secure. Because of the late hours they kept, the men arranged to stay at the inn. But Tony Caseletta, whose wife and child had lodgings in Wilmington, made the journey with Captain Harper as often as possible to be with them.

On the morning of April 23, 1882, according to a newspaper account of what followed that day, Tony kissed his wife and child goodbye at the dock in Wilmington and waved to them from the deck of the *Passport* as it headed downriver for Southport. The trip was uneventful. That afternoon, with time on his hands before the evening dance, Tony accepted an invitation to take a sail around Bald Head Island with his fellow musicians. Since none were seamen, they were probably accompanied by the owner of the boat, but the details of the excursion are sketchy and based on hearsay. Perhaps they took their fishing lines along. They had plenty of time before the evening's festivities, and fishing was good in that location.

The boat was well ballasted and in sound condition; the weather was gorgeous. A gentle breeze caused slight ripples over an otherwise mirrorlike surface on the water. There was no explanation then, nor has there ever been for what happened next. The boat sank. Some said it went straight down rather than capsizing, and that later, visitors to the scene of the accident could look down into the water and observe the sail unfurled, swinging back and forth with the motion of the waves. Though everyone else escaped unharmed, Tony was drowned. His body was recovered soon afterward and buried beneath a stone monument that marks the spot to this day in the Old Smithville Burying Grounds in Southport. The stone reads simply "ANTONIO CASELETTA, BORN 1863, DIED AUGUST 23, 1882."

*   *   *

That should have been the end of the story, but instead it was the beginning. Maybe it was because Tony was only nineteen when his life ended so abruptly, or maybe because of his obsessive attachment to the beloved harp which he played so beautifully, whatever the reason, local lore reveals that Tony returned. While no one is quite sure when he was first heard playing his harp again in the old inn, he has been there for as long as anyone can remember.

Mary Stuart Callari, whose family has owned the property (in later years known as the Brunswick Inn) since 1949, remembers hearing stories of the ghost before they moved in. Her first experience with Tony came in the early fifties when she was in high school. "I was coming home after basketball practice one night. Both my parents were still at work. As I walked up to the house, I thought how big and dark it seemed. I was uneasy about going in alone, but just as I started up the steps lights went on in the living room and kitchen, then room by room all over the house. When I got inside no one was there. The strangest thing was that there were no light switches back then. In fact, even today, the lights have to be turned on by a pull chain from a light fixture in the center of the room. I knew it was

Tony, but somehow, I was not afraid. I felt that he was protecting me."

Stuart Callari's mother, Alice Arrington, who lived there until her death in 1993, heard the ghost many times. She heard his music and also his footsteps walking around the home's spectacular rotunda and continuing down the circular stairway. The ghost was one of her favorite subjects and she used to entertain guests with tales of his antics.

Mrs. Callari, who also has listened to Tony's harp, described the music as "melodic in a strange way. It sounds like a tune, though nothing you could hum. It is rather metallic. When you hear it and follow the sound to where you think it is—it is no longer there. It always sounds off in the distance."

In the days before the house was air-conditioned, Mrs. Callari recalled summertime visits with her children. "The windows would all be open. Sometimes a storm would wake me in the middle of the night. I would get up to shut the windows, but Tony would have already shut them. At other times, the wind would change and it would get cool during the night. I'd get up to get blankets to cover the kids, and when I'd get there they would already be covered up."

Another strange incident happened during a summer vacation when both she and her sister, Pat Pittenger, and their families were visiting. Mrs. Callari was pregnant at the time and being close to term was unable to climb the stairs, so she was given a downstairs bedroom. "I couldn't get to sleep. I kept hearing lots of noise—it got so noisy it woke up Kerry, my young son. It sounded like the house was full of people walking around upstairs, just overhead. Finally, I realized that I was in the only room on the first floor with no room above it." Everyone else was asleep!

In the early fifties, Dr. B. W. Wells, a noted botanist from Raleigh, who owned the Stuart House on the waterfront just below the Brunswick Inn, became interested in the ghost. He arranged for some colleagues of his, professors associated with the parapsychology department at Duke University, to come down and investigate the ghost. The scientists spent several nights in the home and reported hearing it, but were never able to come up with anything conclusive concerning the ghost.

Mrs. Callari says that to her knowledge "the ghost has never manifested itself to anyone visually—it's always been in actions." One guest at the home claimed to have seen Tony, but Mrs. Callari believes that was only because he was determined to see something no matter what. She is not convinced the sighting actually occurred.

Stuart Callari's husband, Barry, who has always been skeptical of the family ghost, has had cause to reconsider during the past several years. "Mother was very sick in the last months before she died and often required attention during the night," Mrs. Callari explained. "Sometimes she would cry out loudly, waking everyone up. At about the same time, the Disney movie, *Spies*, was being filmed in the house, and there was mass confusion most of the time. Early one morning, about 1:15, I was awakened by a loud crash that sounded like someone had turned over the china closet—dishes breaking and glasses, an unmistakable sound. My husband and I were asleep at opposite ends of the house, but we both heard it." When the Callaris went downstairs to investigate, nothing had been disturbed. Everything was in its proper place. On two successive nights at exactly the same time, the crashing sound occurred as before, with the same results. "The only thing we could figure was that Tony, in all the confusion, was reacting in kind."

Another time, a crashing sound was heard and the picture that hung over the mantel in the library was found on the floor in the hallway. A similar occurrence took place in the bedroom. "The family dog who sleeps there always wakes up and growls when Tony comes into the room, then realizing it is Tony, he wags his tail and crawls back into bed," Mrs. Callari said. One night, going through his usual ritual, the dog woke her. Sensing something out of the ordinary, she got up to check, and found that the mantel over the fireplace in her bedroom had been swept clean of all the pictures that were there. They lay unbroken on the floor.

In mid-1995, the house was for sale. With more than 7,000 square feet it was larger than the Callaris needed since their children are grown. When asked if she thought Tony would continue to be there once the house was sold, Mrs Callari replied without hesitation. "Oh absolutely! He'll be here. I don't think he attaches to people. This is his home. He'll stay with the house."

The Night Mama Struggled With the Ghost

Joan Kaiser

> *"Ghosts were created when*
> *the first man woke in the night."*
> Sir James Matthew Barrie
> 1860-1937

The Night Mama Struggled
With the Ghost

It happened in the early 1920s.
Mama always started the story that way.
I was working at the Coast Line Railroad and living in the Magnolia Apartments, that big old three-story house in downtown Wilmington on Fifth Street, near the fountain. The house was built in the 1800s, and I had always heard it was haunted.   In fact, before I moved in, I was told that a young man from the Carolina Apartments next door had moved out because of the ghost. At the time, though, he didn't know it was a ghost. It seems each evening when he went to a table by his window to turn on a lamp, he looked over at the Magnolia Apartments, and she was there.
Mama would pause just long enough to let the tension build, and then she would continue.
Each night a woman dressed in a filmy white dress stood at the second-story window opposite his and beckoned to him as if she were in distress. He tried to ignore it, but finally he just couldn't. He went to the superintendent of

the Magnolia Apartments to complain. The superintendent took him to the second floor and showed him that the apartment in question was vacant. It had been vacant for several weeks. The young man could not believe it. He was almost in shock. The manager of the Carolina Apartments went over the next day to complain. He told the superintendent that the man had moved out. He said it was not the first time such a thing had happened, and that he was getting tired of losing good tenants!"

I asked Mama then if she hadn't been afraid to live there knowing that, and she laughed.

I've always believed in ghosts, but I've never been afraid of them. I loved living there. I was hoping to see one myself. Actually the ghost appeared sooner than I expected, though not to me.

The Clarks lived on the first floor. They were as nice as they could be. George worked with a local insurance company. His wife's name was Sarah. I saw them often when I was leaving for work or coming in at night, and we always stopped awhile just to chat. Sometimes we ran into each other at the Dixie Cafe on Princess Street. I ate there most every night, and they did too. You could buy meal tickets for the week back then, and it was cheaper to do it that way.

I think that was one reason the Clarks liked the location of the apartment house as much as I did, because it was right in the heart of downtown and convenient to everything. They certainly had no intention of moving. That is, until one New Year's Eve when they had an experience that changed everything.

Mama stopped again, knowing we were dying to hear

more. Then she went on with the story.

I came downstairs early in the morning on New
Year's Day. The door to the Clarks' apartment was wide
open, and that seemed strange. I couldn't help noticing the
two of them inside packing. Sarah saw me and waved me in.
Suitcases were open, and she was throwing clothes in as fast
as she could, not even stopping to fold them. I asked her
what on earth was going on. "You're not moving out, are
you?" She looked frantic when she answered me. I noticed
then that she hadn't put on any makeup, and her hair was a
mess. She was always neat as a pin, so I knew something
must really be wrong.

"I'll never spend another night in this house," Sarah
said.

"Last night we returned home from a New Year's Eve
Party at the Cape Fear Country Club. It was late, and we
were very tired. I was impatient as George bent over to put
the key in the door; I just wanted to get in and go to bed.
He turned the knob, and the door had barely opened, when
I saw this figure of a woman, dressed in a thin, filmy, white
gown glide from the room. She was transparent...you could
see her, but you could see right through her too. She seemed
to float up the stairs. It all happened in a split second. I
screamed! George turned to me. He was as white as a sheet,
and he said, 'My God, Sarah, did you see it too?' I have
never been so frightened in my life."

Sarah went on to tell me that they went into the
apartment and immediately started to pack. They had been
up all night. Neither one of them could go to sleep after
that experience. "If I were you, Ann Lou, I'd move out
too." Those were her last words to me. By the time I came

home later in the day, the Clarks were gone; their apartment was completely empty.

I must admit I was shaken up a bit, but I knew I couldn't find another place for the same price that I liked as well. And, to tell the truth, I kinda wanted to see the ghost for myself. So I stayed.

Several months later I came in from work one evening with two of my friends, Alice and Eloise Charles. They were sisters and shared an apartment across the hall from mine on the third floor. They both worked at the Coast Line too, and we had walked home together. We wanted to get freshened up a bit, then we were going over to the Dixie to eat. It was ironic that our conversation on the way upstairs was about the Clarks and the ghost, although we thought about it every time we climbed those stairs. I remember Alice scoffing, "I wouldn't believe in ghosts if I saw one with my own eyes." Just about the time Alice said that, we reached the top of the stairs. It was a little dark in the hallway, but you could still see.

Eloise told Alice to shut up. Alice and I weren't afraid, but Eloise was scared to death of ghosts. She had been uneasy ever since the Clarks moved out.

We knew for certain what was coming next, but every-time, we held our breaths, and waited fearfully to hear it again. Then Mama said...

You remember that old daybed we used to have? Well, I had just bought that and those two Windsor rockers, and the mahogany desk that's in the living room now. I was so proud of having my own things and my apartment looked so pretty.

Mama was doing it again....delaying the story just to

make us more anxious. We begged her to keep on. So she did.

Well anyway, by this time we had come to the door of my apartment. Alice and Eloise roomed right across the hall from me, and they walked on past me. As I reached for my doorknob, I suddenly had a strange, cold feeling, as if some unseen presence were there too. The doorknob turned with no problem, but I couldn't push open the door.

I called to the sisters to come and help me. "It's the ghost!" I yelled. I wasn't joking, but they thought I was, and they started laughing. "It really is the ghost," I yelled again.

"I mean it, someone is holding this door, and they won't let me in." Sure enough, we each tried in turn to push open the door, but it wouldn't budge; it would open just wide enough to see into the room, but it wouldn't go any farther.

Alice said, "Ann Lou, I'll bet it's your brother, Lindon, trying to scare us." I thought maybe it might be too, so we all called out, "All right, Lindon, the joke's over, we know it's you." We didn't hear a sound. The door was still open just a crack. By this time, Alice and Eloise were both beginning to get very frightened, and I was getting angry. We decided to all push against it at the same time. We counted to three and shoved as hard as we could. The door still would not budge. It felt as if someone were pushing against it from the other side.

"That's it," I told them, "I'm going downstairs to get the superintendent."

"No, you stay here; I'll go." Alice said. I think she volunteered so she wouldn't have to stand there. I'm sure she thought the ghost might decide to show itself, and in spite of what she'd said earlier, she wasn't ready for that! Eloise was right behind her!

In a few minutes, they were both back with the superintendent. He reached for the doorknob and pushed. We couldn't believe what we saw! The door swung wide open just as easy as you please. That's all there was to it, but there was no doubt in my mind what had been pushing against it from the other side!

We breathed a sigh of relief. We must have heard that story a zillion times, but every time we were just sure that ghost was gonna reach out and grab Mama. It never did though, thank goodness!

A Host of Historic Hauntings

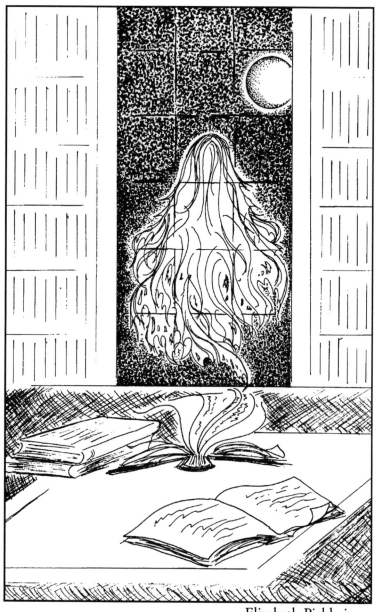

Elizabeth Picklesimer

*"From ghoulies and ghosties and long-leggety beasties
And things that go bump in the night,
Good Lord, deliver us."*
"The Cornish Litany"
Anonymous

A HOST OF HISTORIC HAUNTINGS

The Library Ghost

Though several Wilmington ghosts have received national attention, only one has ever been listed in a book called *The Ghostly Register*, a guide to haunted buildings in the United States, published by Contemporary Books of Chicago. That ghost (or ghosts) haunts the New Hanover County Library, namely the Local History Room, which is presided over by state and local history librarian, Beverly Tetterton.

Mrs. Tetterton was the first to become aware of the rustle of pages, soft footsteps across the carpeted floor when no one was there, and the sounds of people putting books on a shelf or knocking against the metal bookshelves, "noises that maybe only a librarian would be familiar with." Often she would hear activity in the stacks, knowing she had just said goodbye to the last person to leave. Sometimes she would lock up at night, only to find the pamphlet cases unlocked the following morning, or a drawer slightly opened and all of the drawers unlocked.

The ghost is not only noisy, it has actually been seen by at least three people on different occasions. Two men who use the historical collection reported seeing the figure of a short woman who strongly resembled a deceased, and much beloved, historian who frequented the library on many occasions. Mrs. Tetterton mentioned the sighting to some of the woman's relatives, and "they laughed and said that would be just like her."

One of the men, who did not want to be identified for fear of being thought deranged by non-believers, saw the ghost first in 1982, and then again in 1983. An article in the *Raleigh News and Observer* quoted him as saying, "I was looking through the top of the shelves, and I could see her over the books. I called her name. She looked at me, then turned real quickly and flew down to the end of the stacks." He rushed to tell Mrs. Tetterton about the encounter. "Those people were white as ghosts themselves," the librarian said after talking with both men.

On another occasion, a local lady reported seeing an apparition as she came around a corner in the stacks. The apparition was a human figure, she maintained, but it faded so quickly that it was impossible to recognize.

It may be that this ghost is one which haunted the previous location of the library, the old Wilmington Light Infantry Armory on Market Street, formerly a private residence belonging to the John Taylor family. Mrs. Tetterton worked there for a short time before the library was moved. She was apprised of the ghost's activities almost as soon as she began work. The reports were mainly of noises, shadows, and footsteps. One night as she sat at the check-out desk, Mrs. Tetterton saw a strange shadow. When she told a co-worker about it, the girl said, "Get your hat and pocketbook and let's get out of here."

There is yet another possible explanation for the specter. It could be the spirit which haunted the house that earlier occupied the site of the present library. Built in the early 1950s by Belks, a regional department store chain, the current building was converted to the public library in 1981 when Belks moved to a suburban mall. The building was constructed where the Woods house, a handsome three-story Italianate structure, once stood. Legend holds that a local man spent his last night in the Woods home before dueling to his death the following day. He was said to be in a state of agitation all night, pacing the floor and agonizing over the possibility of his death. From that time until the old house was destroyed, his footsteps continued to echo in that bedroom.

Mrs. Tetterton points out that the Local History Room is thought to be in the approximate location of the haunted room in the Woods house. Many books belonging to the Woods family were donated to the library and may now be found in the historical wing. "I don't know that much about ghosts," Mrs. Tetterton said. "Someone told me they haunt pieces of property, buildings and things. It was our theory that when we moved the old books here, something came with them." But that doesn't explain why the library visitor seems to be a woman when the ghost in the Woods house was a man.

Unlike ghosts who undertake their scary escapades

in the silence of the night, the library's apparitions are best heard in the morning. Despite that, the janitorial staff cleans the area housing the North Carolina collection early, preferring to be on the first floor after the library is closed. "I can't blame them," Mrs. Tetterton says. However, she's not sure the janitors have anything to worry about anymore. She believes that all the attention and publicity the ghosts received during the late1980s may have scared them away. All has been quiet in recent years, and no one has seen any manifestations lately. It's even a bit lonely without them. They somehow seemed to belong there.

The Basket Case

The Basket Case, a gift shop in the city's historic Cotton Exchange, boasts among its customers a spectral couple who appear without warning to shop and then disappear as suddenly as they came.

The Basket Case is located in the Dahnhardt Building which in the late 1800s housed a three-story mariner's saloon and inn. Jean Hansen, owner of The Basket Case, thinks the couple might be former patrons of the pub who occasionally stop by for a drink. She first remembered seeing them some years ago. "I was standing outside talking to some customers, and I opened the door for the couple. When I went inside, no one was there." There is only one entrance to this shop, and Mrs. Hansen was standing right beside it!

Another time, the store was filled with shoppers, and the couple walked in and began to look around and smile. Mrs. Hansen said, "Gee, I wonder if those people need some help." When she sent her sister (who also works in the shop) over to help them, they had disappeared. Again, no one had left through the only door to the shop.

Mrs. Hansen is so convinced of the specters' reality that she keeps an old photograph from a magazine pinned to the wall behind her check-out counter. The couple in the photograph are dressed in beige and the picture is fairly colorless, reminding Mrs. Hansen of her ghostly visitors. "You don't think about it until after it's happened, and then you realize...they were here again."

Robert Blanton

The Bellamy Mansion

Built in 1859 by Dr. John D. Bellamy, the Bellamy Mansion is one of the most magnificent houses in the city. The mansion is an extravagant mix of architectural styles characteristic of pre-Civil War residences. Stately Corinthian columns give the home a grace and beauty that is enhanced by the distinctive moldings and balconies which decorate its facade. The family of Dr. Bellamy had scarcely gotten settled there when war became a threat to the city, and in 1865, Federal troops under the command of General Hawley took possession of the house for the general's headquarters. Mrs. Bellamy was appalled by the accounts passed on to her of all kinds of debauchery and disgraceful activities taking place in her beautiful new home. Indeed, the home was in a shambles when it was returned to the family in September of 1865, only seven months after it was occupied by Union soldiers.

Not long after the Bellamys moved back in, servants who lived in the outbuildings began to tell stories about fearsome spirits in the main house. Several claimed to have seen a skeleton in the basement area and were terrified of going near that part of the house again. In truth they had seen one. But it was not the supernatural manifestation they imagined.

The troublemaker in this case was Willie, one of the Bellamy sons. Willie had read medicine under his father and then had left home to attend a medical college. He was given a room in the basement for his office. This room was formerly used as an ironing room by the servants. His sister, Ellen Douglas Bellamy, recalled in her memoirs that when

Willie returned from school in New York, he brought with him an articulated skeleton which he had used in his classes. He took great delight in scaring the servants with the skeleton then hiding it again. From time to time, he laid the horrid thing on the ironing board (which resembled a coffin lid) and left it there until it had accomplished its purpose. Some poor unsuspecting servant always managed to walk unwittingly into Willie's trap. No doubt Willie enjoyed his role in keeping the "spirits" of the basement alive and well!

In later years there were different stories. Passers-by, on occasion, told of seeing an older couple in old-fashioned dress, silhouetted in one of the upstairs windows, though no one fitting their descriptions could possibly have been there at the time. It has never been determined who the two might have been. Reports of their appearance have declined in recent years. Sometimes visitors to the house have claimed to hear the faint sounds of young voices or the laughter of a woman, but nothing clearly discernible.

The interior of the house certainly lends itself to "spirits," with its monumental maze of rooms, ranging from the full basement to a belvedere atop the structure, which offers a stunning view of the city. But the Bellamys' numerous children and the mischief they concocted probably accounted for many of the stories of strange happenings in the house.

The last surviving child, Ellen, died there in 1946. Following her death, the home passed through a series of heirs until 1972 when Bellamy Mansion Incorporated was formed to preserve it. The cost of restoration was enormous, and the preservation efforts foundered, but finally in 1989, Bellamy Mansion Incorporated combined their funds with those of the Historic Preservation Foundation of North Carolina, and the restoration is currently ongoing.

The Bellamy Mansion Museum, as it is now called, is the pride of a community steeped in history, and its stories live on in the animated words of volunteer tour guides who clearly love their work. If the guides should hear voices occasionally, or catch a fleeting glimpse of a child's smiling face peeping around the corner of the children's playroom, they don't mind—it's all part of the job.

The Burgwin-Wright House

This historic house at the corner of Third and Market Streets is thought by many to be the oldest home in Wilmington. The site was purchased in 1744 for the construction of a jail, and a map by C. J. Sauthier in 1769 shows the "gaol," a masonry building that later became part of the foundations of the present structure. That structure has long been known as the "Cornwallis House," based on the tradition that Lord Cornwallis and his staff occupied it when the city was captured by the British during the Revolutionary War. Although there has never been positive proof that Lord Cornwallis himself stayed there, the likelihood is strong. It is known for certain that British forces did commandeer the property.

Many have claimed that the spirits of tortured souls, imprisoned by Cornwallis in the dungeon beneath the cellar floor, remained to haunt the house. And some years ago, a local citizen had a strangely unsettling experience there.

In the early days of the city's Azalea Festival, a well-known radio and television personality from Virginia was visiting Wilmington as an honored guest. Being a bit of a history and antique buff, she was charmed with the historic downtown area and was delighted when she was invited for a tour of the Cornwallis house. One of the ladies in the community who shared the celebrity's interest in antiquities was invited, along with her husband, to accompany the celebrity.

Met at the door by a docent who was well versed in the history of the house, the three toured the first floor rooms and then were led up the stairs to a bedroom at the top of the stairs which faced the street. The docent opened the door and stepped aside to let the three enter. This was before the days when the home was furnished as completely as it is now, and there was nothing in the room but a spinning wheel on the hearth and a chaise longue alongside the wall. The local lady, acting as hostess to the city's guest, was the first to enter the room, and she was startled to see the spinning wheel begin to turn very slowly. As the group watched, the spinning wheel turned faster and faster until the spokes were no longer visible. The hostess' husband tried to explain the phenomenon by saying that the draft from the open door had started the motion of the wheel.

At that, the docent went over to the spinning wheel, which by then had ceased its turning as abruptly as it had begun. She told the three visitors that she had never before seen the spinning wheel turn. It had always been stuck, she said, and because of its age the docents had not tried to force it for fear of breaking it. She was astounded by what she had seen and immediately tried to start the wheel spinning again, whereupon she realized that it would not budge. It was stuck fast, just as it had always been. In the meantime, the local lady had moved closer to the spinning wheel. She later revealed that she seemed to hear a voice in her mind saying clearly, "It's hidden in the wall. It's hidden in the wall." No one else had heard anything at all. The three promptly left the docent and the house behind, feeling that something truly supernatural and frightening had occurred.

The hostess was so shaken by the incident that she decided to write an account of what had happened and send it to the parapsychology department at Duke University. She received a reply from that institution confirming her suspicions that what she and the others had seen was a true ghostly manifestation. It was many years before she could be persuaded to enter the old house again. When she did, she noticed that the spinning wheel had been moved to the old kitchen in back of the house.

Another story, not so much a ghost story as an intriguing mystery, is one which has fascinated area residents as well as tourists for many years. According to this legend (and there are countless variations), one of Lord Cornwallis' officers used the diamond ring he wore to scratch the name of his true love on a pane of glass in one of the windows of the house. Judge Joshua Wright and his family lived in the home during the time of the British occupation. Some accounts said the young lady was actually one of Judge Wright's young daughters, who had fallen for the gallant enemy officer. But another story, attributed to Miss Rowe Wiggins, who occupied the house until her death in 1930, indicated that the soldier's girlfriend was someone else.

As Miss Wiggins told it, she was surprised one day to

find an "attractive young Englishman" at her door. The Englishman informed Miss Wiggins that he had a letter in his possession written by his ancestor, to the girl that ancestor later married. The letter described the Cornwallis house in detail and told how the officer had scratched his sweetheart's name on the glass during his stay there in 1781. The young Englishman asked if he might look for the window pane. Upon checking the rooms, no such pane of glass could be found. He then asked Miss Wiggins if the sashes had ever been replaced, and she remembered having seen some old windows stacked in the basement. They made their way to the basement, and, sure enough, the window was found with the name clearly etched upon the pane. The young man was so thrilled that Miss Wiggins gave him the entire sash. It was promptly crated and shipped to his home in England, where it may well be to this day.

Miss Wiggins said the Englishman had also questioned her about an old tunnel (that was mentioned in the letter) that ran from the lower cellar to the river, but no tunnel could be found. There had always been rumors of such a tunnel, reputedly used as an escape route by some of the more fortunate prisoners who had located it. Some years later, when the new city sewer was being put in, the tunnel was actually discovered.

For more than two hundred years, this grand old house has seen a continuing saga unfold. Serving as headquarters for British officers in the Revolutionary War, and seized again by Federal officers during the Civil War, the house was rented by the city during World War II and outfitted for the use of military officers once again, though this time, fortunately, not for the enemy! Owned now by The

North Carolina Society of Colonial Dames and restored to its former elegance, the house is open to the public. Is it any wonder that visitors to this place seem to feel the phantoms and to hear the whispers of the past in every room?

The Purnell-Empie House

"Well, we do have a ghost here. And she's mischievous, you see," Hannah Block says of the home she lives in at 319 S. Front Street. " I had a guest once who swore she had seen our ghost sitting on her bed during the night, but I've never seen her and my housemate, Mary, has never seen her. We put things down and go for maybe a week trying to find things, and we know daggone well we haven't misplaced them. Mary will say, 'Hannah, I know I put the keys here,' and I'll say, 'You know, Mary, I believe you. It's Miss Empie again." The name is in honor of one of the earlier mistresses of the home.

Mrs. Block loves to talk about ghosts and admits there may be more than one reason for the house being haunted. On a window in the dining room of her home, the name Blanche is scratched across the old glass pane, much like the British soldier scratched the name on a pane at the Cornwallis house. "I want to tell you a sad story," Mrs. Block said. She pointed to a neighboring house almost close enough to reach out and touch. "The Chadbourn family lived next door there during the Civil War. They left and went to the mountains to get away from the fighting. In the fall, they returned on the train. They had a seventeen-year-old son and whether the girl was sixteen or eighteen, I can't tell you. Anyway, they both got typhoid fever and they were quarantined. Their friends used to come to this house and stand at the window and visit them by waving and talking through the window. Of course, the two teen-agers did die from the fever. Blanche was the daughter. One of her friends etched her name there." Mrs. Block thinks the tragic circumstances surrounding Blanche's death have caused her spirit to linger.

"I found this house to be a very historic house when we began to restore it," Mrs. Block recalled. She and her late husband, Charles, were largely responsible for the movement to renovate the treasured old homes in the historic district, and her home was the first.

"It was two houses made into one with thirty-four rooms. The rear section was a house in the back that Governor Dudley had built for his daughter. During World War II, the Boneys owned it. Back then you couldn't find an apartment for love nor money, so they made this house into six apartments. Mrs. Ida Kellam, a local historian who is now deceased, said the kitchen dated back to 1790. The back of the house was built in 1835. This part of the house was built in 1859. The two were joined by a breezeway.

"We hired an architect and in order to safely restore the house he had to jack it up and dig down to lay a cement foundation. When they dug down, they found human bones and beside the bones lay an old military button. I didn't know what to make of it, but I had a friend who was head of the FBI here, so I called him and he came and got the bones and sent them off for testing, and the report came back saying that the bones were probably from the Civil War period." It could be that the ghosts which haunt the house are from that era. "They are good ghosts as far as I'm concerned," Mrs. Block said.

She also discovered that the house was used as a hospital during the Civil War. Maybe the bones were from amputees, or perhaps they belonged to the wounded soldiers who died in the house. Mrs. Block still has the military button, but she declined an offer from the FBI man to give back the bones.

The Captain Cooke House

Nestled cozily behind a white picket fence at 321 S. Fourth Street is a quaint cottage known as the Captain Cooke house. Its pale green shutters have little sailboats cut out at the top, appropriate decor since the house reputedly has been owned by two of Wilmington's most famous sea captains. The house certainly doesn't look haunted, but it is.

For as long as anyone can remember, occupants of the home have heard footsteps in the upstairs hall. The current owners, Herman and Suzanne Smith, are no exception. "Between two and five in the morning you can hear footsteps right outside our bedroom door," Mrs. Smith said.

"It's not scary, but I get up to check on them, and there's nothing there."

One night when Mrs. Smith's brother was visiting, he slept in the bedroom next to hers. Early the next morning he greeted his sister, mentioned that he had heard her walking around during the night, and said he hoped that she had not been ill. She admitted she had been restless, but had never gotten out of bed. It must have been the ghost!

The Smiths also have another problem that has plagued many of the residents of the Cooke house—the light bulbs. "The entire house has been rewired, but we are constantly having to replace the light bulbs," Mrs. Smith said. "Even the long lasting bulbs don't last!"

Although the Smiths have never seen the ghost, one family member who gets strange vibrations when she visits thinks she may have. Earlier residents of the home have told of actually seeing a manifestation. And one couple who lived there seemed to feel a presence from time to time.

Many think the spirit is that of Captain William Cooke, who is reputed to have built the house in 1784. Commissioned as captain of the Revenue Cutter *Diligence* by President George Washington in 1791, Captain Cooke made quite a name for himself locally when he captured a French privateer and claimed a cache of gold for the United States government.

It was said that he was not a popular man because of his doggedness in going after the privateers. Some believe that accounts for Captain Cooke's mysterious disappearance in 1796. No one was ever able to discover what happened to him. But it has long been thought that he might have come back to haunt the old house. Perhaps, they say, he's returned to find the gold reportedly stashed on the property or in a tunnel rumored to run from this house to the river. Mr. Smith admits to digging a few exploratory holes in the backyard from time to time—just in case.

Some think the ghost might be that of Captain Silas Martin who once owned the house, or his unfortunate children who died tragic early deaths.* Others are convinced it is William Anderson's spirit. Anderson was a respected jeweler who occupied the house in the 1860s. An excellent silversmith, Mr. Anderson was unfortunately not a good businessman. Heavily in debt and in very poor health, Anderson hanged himself—tradition says—from a tree in his own backyard.

But the weight of opinion is that the ghost is that of Captain Cooke. "At least one person claims to have seen him," writes Florence Kern, a historian who wrote a history of Captain Cooke's ship, "a shadowy figure dressed in blue, enveloped in a blue haze."

* For more on this, see the chapter on Oakdale Cemetery.

Maggie

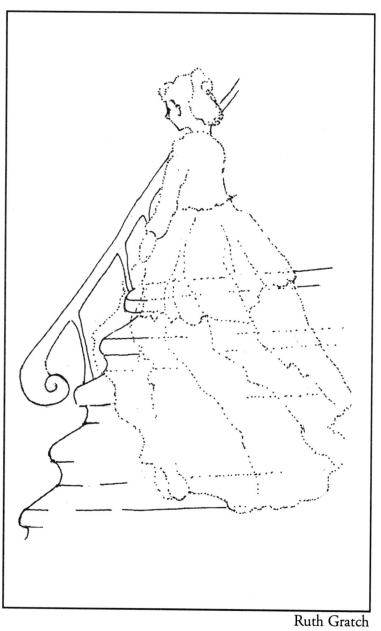

Ruth Gratch

"None shall part us from each other,
One in life and death are we."
Sir William Schwenck Gilbert
1836-1911

Maggie

The house at 117 S. Fourth Street, an impressive Queen
Anne style residence, was built by George W. Williams for his
daughter, Maggie W. Holladay, in 1889. Maggie's husband,
William W. Holladay, designed the exterior of the house. Just
three weeks before it was completed Maggie died giving birth to
her second child, Marguerite. The grieving widower moved into
the house when it was finished, with his two little girls, Nannie
and Marguerite. Shortly thereafter, strange stories began to be
told of a ghost, resembling the dead woman, which appeared to
haunt the second floor bedrooms and stairway of the home,
checking on the motherless children. The house has changed
owners a number of times, and with each successive owner the
stories of Maggie have persisted. One such account was told to
me by the current owner, Orrell Jones.

I grew up on the corner of Fourth and Orange so I
knew about the ghost long before I ever moved here. My
grandmother, Bessie Orrell, used to play bridge in the house.
There were many times when she'd tell me about Maggie
pushing the cards off of the table. She also said that very
often all of the ladies playing cards could hear the swish of

Maggie's taffeta petticoats as she strolled around the table watching the game.

The legend has always been that Maggie's ghost primarily checks the bedrooms upstairs making sure that her children are all right. In March of 1986 when we bought the house from the Guthries, they told us that frequently they would hear noises upstairs. They would go up to the middle bedroom above the music room, and there they would find toys that Maggie appeared to have dropped in the middle of the room. They did not report ever having seen the ghost, however.

Our first Christmas in the house, we were hanging ornaments on the tree in the living room. As we watched in amazement, it seemed as if someone were touching the ornaments and the branches would dip down, from one place to another all over the tree. Our eight year old son, David, was petrified, and said, "Mommy it's the ghost!"

Between 1987 and 1989, all three of us—my husband, Alan, David, and myself—at different times would see her in the middle of the night in the upstairs hall. The first time I saw her, I had gotten up and started down the hall to the bathroom. There was a night light on in the hallway and one in the bathroom, so it wasn't completely dark. When I realized it was Maggie, I woke Alan up, and he came out into the hall and saw her too. We always saw just the back of her, never the front. She seemed to be in silhouette...all in black...with hoop skirts, no real details such as hair or hands, just like a silhouette is the only way I can describe her. From the very first, we never had any negative feelings about her. She seemed harmless, and we have never been afraid of her. We have always had small dogs in the house, but they never have been disturbed by her presence either.

David saw her once, looking into the master bedroom. Even he was not frightened of her after that first incident with the Christmas tree. We all just sort of accepted her as part of the family. But, it was only during that two year period that we actually saw her materialize and not once since then.

Many times we experienced toys and books of David's being moved around. Sometimes we found them sitting in the middle of the floor of the second bedroom just as the Guthries had described.

Between 1990 and 1992, Alan and I went through a period when we thought about selling the house and moving to another state. Every time we went out of town to look at property our security system went off several times during our absence. There was never any indication of a break-in. Nothing was ever amiss in the house. When we went on vacation, it never happened. It was only on those trips for the purpose of looking at other property. I am absolutely convinced that it was Maggie, upset because we might leave. I got real neurotic about it. I even told Alan and David not to say a word about it in the house when we were planning one of our trips, so she wouldn't know!

In 1992, we started a huge renovation on the house. There were all sorts of workmen in the house and lots of confusion. When we first started to do the renovations all three of us had a sensation of someone walking past us on the stairs—like a current of air—no footsteps, but definitely the sound of rustling petticoats.

Since 1993, when the work was completed, I have not seen, heard, or experienced anything at all from her. I am sure she was satisfied with everything that has been done. It's almost as if finally the house is back in good shape, and she is pleased and happy and ready to let go and say, okay, do whatever you want to do.

I always felt her presence very strongly until that time. I really did feel that she was concerned about the well-being of the house. I don't think she is here anymore. Whatever she was worried about seems now to have been put to rest.

In the Spirit
of Things

Joan Kaiser

> *"The most beautiful thing we can experience is the mysterious."*
>
> Albert Einstein
> 1879-1955

In The Spirit of Things

This story was told to me by a dear friend, Joyce Cooper. It is a true story, and one I thought worth sharing. I tell it here as she told it to me.

I have never felt afraid at all, even though I realized soon after I moved here that the house was haunted. In fact, I much prefer life in a haunted house to living in one that is not haunted.

I bought the house in November of 1988. The address of the house is 15 N. 15th Street, and as it turned out I moved in on November 15. Those numbers seem to be significant for me. I just loved this house from the very beginning. I was looking for a condo on the beach, but I ended up with an old house built in 1903. I think I was meant to be here.

Several weeks after I moved in my sister and brother-in-law came to visit. I put them in the blue room upstairs. My bedroom is on the first floor, so it was the first time anyone had spent the night upstairs. I went to bed early because I was working the next day, but they stayed up late to watch TV. After they went up to bed, turned out the lights and lay down to go to sleep, they heard a moaning sound. It was enough to make them get up and start looking out of the windows, and then it stopped. So they got back into bed and turned off the lights. It started again—this moaning.

Finally, Mary Ann, my sister, got up and came downstairs to see if there was something wrong with me, even though the noise did not seem to be coming from that direction. I was sound asleep. My brother-in-law, who did not believe in this kind of stuff, became a believer that night with all that moaning. Eventually, though, they went on to sleep. The next morning they couldn't wait to tell me that I had a haunted upstairs. I laughed it off. "I stay in the house by myself," I told them, "and I have never been bothered with anything." But it made me wonder.

The next incident was a long time after that, the Wednesday night my writers' group came over. Instead of having our regular meeting—it was during the summer—we had decided to try using a Ouija Board in the blue room to see what might be going on with the spirit. There were four of us. Blonnie and I worked the Ouija Board, and it moved around. Blonnie had never done a Ouija Board before. It moved around so much that she said if she hadn't known me as well as she did, she'd think I was pushing it. We kept on asking questions and the first word it spelled out was "Help," which just sent shivers all over me. After that it moved around a lot, but it never spelled out anything else. Maggi was writing everything down, but nothing made any sense. It was hot upstairs, so we quit and just gave up. We went down and played the piano and had some drinks, then everyone went home.

That Friday morning I woke up and was on my way to the bathroom when I saw a book lying in the middle of the floor beside the bookcase in the hall. None of the other books were disturbed. It was a book about games, and I remembered that Blonnie had said on Wednesday night that she felt the spirit was either a child or a very playful spirit. I got all excited about that, so I left the book on the floor and went to work. I told my friend, Deb, at work. Deb already knew about the other incidents.

"She's playing with you," Deb said. "You went up and disturbed her and tried to communicate with her, now she's probably trying to communicate with you."

Saturday afternoon I was taking a nap on the sofa. When I got up and went out into the hall, there was another book in the middle of the floor, this one about TV game shows. The only two books I have in the house on games had now ended up on the floor. I took pictures of the hallway showing they were there and then replaced the books on the shelf. For a long time after that nothing happened.

My friend, Maggi, was visiting in November. She stays with me when she comes to Wilmington to teach a class. We're both writers so she understood when I told her I'd probably be up writing most of the night. She was very tired and she went on to bed—in the blue room. The next morning she came down and said, "Joyce, did you come to my room last night and talk to me?"

"No," I said, "I was in the next room writing on my computer, and I was trying to be very quiet so I wouldn't wake you." Actually I had never even gone to bed. She said she could have sworn that someone came in and talked to her and said that I was working on my novel—even told her what chapters I was working on. That was the part which made us feel that it wasn't just a dream, because the chapters she mentioned were the ones I had worked on all night. It was really weird.

Many months later, my mother brought my aunt to visit. Mother stayed a few days and then left my aunt with me. A friend of my aunt was supposed to come, spend the night with us and take Aunt Mattie Lee back to Georgia the next morning. The woman arrived and put her bag in the blue room. She came downstairs, and the three of us went out to sit on the porch and have a glass of wine. My aunt mentioned the ghost to her friend. That didn't seem to bother the woman, but then Aunt Mattie Lee told her about the Ouija Board. All of a sudden this woman went wild and started talking about such things being evil and the work of the devil. I was stunned.

About that time I heard a loud crash. I got up to see what might have fallen and also to check on supper. I didn't see anything at first, so I went on into the kitchen. When I came out, I could see that a heavy picture had fallen off of the wall onto the dining room floor, right under the blue room. Nothing was broken, not the glass nor the wire. I just figured the spirit was mad at the woman and had decided to interrupt her tirade. I hung the picture again and forgot about it.

Soon afterward I decided to see a psychic. I wanted to know if she could tell me anything about my ghostly inhabitant. Immediately when she saw me, she said, "there is a spirit in your house. She lived on the land before the current house was built, years and years ago, and was very close with the family who lived there too. One day the family went out to try to get food and left her in charge of all their valuables. Some raiders came and killed the woman and stole all the family's goods. The woman has not been able to rest since, knowing that she was unable to protect the family. Now her spirit is protective of whoever lives in the house."

The psychic told me several ways to try and put the spirit at ease and release her. But I am selfish, and as I said earlier, I rather like having her here to take care of things. I don't know if what the psychic said was true, but it was interesting.

Another friend came to visit me a short time later. I had never told this friend, who is rather psychic herself, about my ghost. She drove down from Raleigh and when she came in the door, the first thing she said to me was, "I sense that you have a spirit in your house, and her name is Helen." How she knew this, I don't know. She knew enough though, without my saying a word, to decide that she would not sleep upstairs, although I have three perfectly good bedrooms there. She always sleeps on the sofa now when she comes to visit.

Since that time I have referred to my spirit by her name, Helen. I am careful when I go into the blue room myself, because one night I went upstairs and turned on the light in the blue room and started to put some sheets in the closet. When I reached out to open the door, I felt something like electricity go all through my body. I put the sheets down and left, but I knew Helen was right there at that moment. My friend, Deb, spent the night in that room a short time ago. I had never told her about the electricity thing, but the next morning she came downstairs and told me it had happened to her. She described it in the same way that I had felt it.

You might think after all this that I would prefer to live somewhere else, but that is the furthest thing from my mind. I feel comfortable with Helen here. When I go to sleep at night, I know she is watching out for me. And when I go out of town on a trip, I always tell her goodbye and ask her to keep an eye on things. I feel that she does, and it suits us both.

The Playful Ghost
of the
Price-Gause House

Elizabeth Picklesimer

"As I was going up the stair
I met a man who wasn't there.
He wasn't there again today.
I wish, I wish he'd stay away."
Hughes Mearns
1875-1965

The Playful Ghost of the Price-Gause House

Not all ghosts are scary. Take, for instance, the friendly fellow who has haunted the Price-Gause house for years. Nowadays, the building houses an architectural firm and the ghost is such a familiar fixture that he regularly gets blamed when a file is missing or something has gone awry. "George did it," is the standard explanation which everyone accepts.

The house at 514 Market Street wasn't always just a place of business. It was built in 1843 by Dr. William Price to accommodate both his medical offices and his family. The offices were in the basement, a rarity in Wilmington, and the family occupied the two stories above it.

Almost as soon as the Price family moved into their new home in 1843, they became aware of strange and unusual occurrences: sounds of footsteps on the spiral stairway, doors opening and closing without warning, odors of cooking food, all completely inexplicable.

The family had surely known when they built there that the site of the home was part of a property formerly known as Gallows Hill, a place for public hangings. More than likely, it also served as a burial ground for the poor wretches who were hanged there and had no one to claim their bodies. It may be that Dr. Price, being a man of science, had no fear of the supernatural and brushed aside warnings that spirits might decide to take up residence in his new home.

One of the most persistent stories about Gallows Hill (which Dr. Price surely had heard) is that an accused thief, a man named James Peckham, was hung in the late 1700s for stealing an expensive purse, even though he protested his innocence to the very end. Supposedly, Peckham continues to search the premises looking for evidence to clear his name of its stigma.

Another story is told of a man who was awaiting execution at Gallows Hill and somehow managed to escape. He ran from the hanging grounds to the house on another section of the property and was taken in by the servants, who took pity on him and hid him. Apparently, the story goes, he was in bad shape from his ordeal and forthwith died, probably in the basement. His spirit came back to stay because the house was the only place where he had ever been treated with kindness.

For some reason, even with the rather gruesome fact of their home's historic setting, the Price family, and later the Gause family, were never frightened by the ghost. Rather, it came to be an accepted part of the house by each generation. Joseph Price, a Captain in the Confederate Navy and son of the original owner, brought his bride to live there. Joseph left the home to his widow whose only living heir, Thomas Gause, Sr., inherited it in 1934 and soon moved his family there. The antics of the ghostly inhabitant increased at once, possibly due to the very able assistance of Mr. Gause's lively youngsters, Thomas Jr. and Mary Frances.

More than half a century later, Mary Frances Gause Oppelt still recalled the ghost as if he'd been a member of the family. "We moved there in 1937, and we lived there the whole time until the house was sold to the Chamber of Commerce in 1968," she said in a 1995 interview. "I think that was when the ghost came to be called George, but we always called him Grandpa."

Mrs. Oppelt was thirteen when the family moved in. She was given the left front bedroom facing Market Street. "There was a wicker rocking chair with a cushion in the bottom that sat in a corner of the room. All of a sudden for no reason you'd hear *creak-creak* and it would just be rocking back and forth, and back and forth. So my brother, who was always very interested in ghostly things, came into my room and took that chair and put it in every place in the room, and it would still rock. It couldn't have been just an unlevel floor as some folks suggested." She grew so used to the phenomenon that she paid it no mind.

Another incident that remained vivid in Mary Frances Gause Oppelt's memory happened to her mother. "Several years after we moved in, a man came to the house. I don't know what you call them, but they come and try to figure what the ghost is—ghost hunters, I reckon. Well anyway, he was in the area writing a book about ghosts, and he had heard about the house. He called up my mother and asked if he could come and try to see if he could find who or what the spirit was. She told him emphatically no. She told the man that we had a very friendly ghost, and she didn't want anyone disturbing him, because he might decide to get unfriendly! There was no way she would let him in that house. He wrote the book and he did mention the stories, but he never got in the house, and my mother never would talk to him either. You'd sorta have to know my mother to fully appreciate that."

Another time some workmen were digging in the side yard putting in a fence and hit something which appeared to be an underground brick wall that extended beneath the foundation of the house. "We never knew what that room was for," Mrs. Oppelt said. "Somebody thought maybe it was a wine cellar. My mother decided that it might be a burial vault and she would not let them dig anymore. They closed it back up and I don't know if anyone has ever opened it or not, but the room is there."

The black housekeeper who worked for the Gause family for many years, and for the Price family before that, had her own experiences with the ghost. "She would complain all the time," Mrs. Oppelt said, "that things were not where she had put them, or that she knew somebody had been in her kitchen. She knew none of us had been, certainly not my mother because she was not a cook. And there was the smell of something cooking when there was no one in the kitchen." (The odor of baked sweet potatoes continues to fill the house on occasion.)

From the time the Gauses moved in they, too, heard the familiar footsteps on the staircase. "Often my brother, Thomas, would get up to check when he heard them, and of course no one was there." Mrs. Oppelt recalled. "Another thing about the footsteps...during the war, my mother rented a room to a man named Frank who worked at the shipyard. Mother would leave the front door unlocked for him, and he was to lock it when he came in. He would also turn off the upstairs hall light. One night I could have sworn I heard Frank come in and come up the stairs. I could see through my bedroom door that the upstairs light was still on, and I thought 'oh, Frank, you dummy, you forgot to turn off the light.' I got up to turn off the light and then wondered if he had locked the front door. I went down and the door wasn't locked, so I locked it. About half an hour later there was a banging and carrying-on at the door, and it was Frank. He had not been home, and when he got there he found he was locked out. That kind of thing happened frequently."

Years later, when Mrs. Oppelt's brother, Thomas Gause, married, he brought his bride, Lynne, to stay at the

house. Her first night in the old house was such a memorable one she wrote an article about her experiences that was published in *The State*. She described it thus. "A chill enveloped the house, although it was late summer. I thought I had solved this problem when I found several patchwork quilts on the shelves of the linen closet and tucked them tightly across the bed before I drifted off to sleep. My slumber was rudely interrupted, when I felt a strong ethereal force pulling the covering from the bed. I awakened Tom, and he told me quietly that this had happened before. I began to believe the tales of the ghost that haunts the old dwelling."

The new Mrs. Gause was treated to other manifestations which the family by now had grown accustomed to. Her bedroom mirror clouded over, but when she reached out to wipe off the steam, the mirror was not even damp. Clouding mirrors happened all the time, upstairs and down. Of course, she also heard the footsteps on the old spiral stairway and saw the wicker rocker rocking by itself. Sometimes the lights would dim and then slowly go out. She learned to be "intrigued, more than frightened."

The most revealing bit of information Mary Frances Gause Oppelt had to share concerned a photograph supposedly taken of the ghost by a Wilmington newspaper photographer in the 1960s. The photograph, clearly showing a ghost on the stairway of the house, had been reproduced in several publications and had come to be accepted as authentic by locals, mainly because the photographer signed an affidavit to that effect.

"That is a complete story," Mrs Oppelt laughed. "It was a put-up job between the photographer and my brother, Tom, who was a writer for the *Star News* for years. I wasn't in on it when it happened and not knowing anything about photography, I don't know how they did it, because it does look exactly like a ghost. But, there was not a word of truth in it!"

Perhaps there is no truth to the photograph, but everyone, including Mrs. Oppelt, is convinced of the authenticity of the gentle poltergeist who inhabits the Price-Gause house.

Today the stately old home is as beautiful as when it was built. The architects have completed an extensive renovation. They have made some structural changes to accommodate their business needs, but they have maintained as much of the historical integrity of the home as they possibly could. The old wide-plank wood floors brought over on a ship from one of the Caribbean Islands and put in with pegs, rather than nails, have been stripped and refinished. The high ceilings and elegant mouldings gleam with fresh paint, the fireplaces are graceful and quaint. Original windows which go all the way to the floor are adorned in an expensive-looking manner, reminiscent of the days when the house was the splendid new residence of one of the city's leading citizens.

No one in the office seems bothered by the ghost, although they have all heard his footsteps and smelled the distinctive odor of pipe tobacco that is characteristic of his spirit. However, one secretary did admit that she wouldn't go down in the basement late at night. "Friendly or not—when I'm up here at 11:00 at night, I don't like to hear anything!"

George (or Grandpa) has been around for over a hundred fifty years. Whereas some ghosts tend to disappear with the passage of time or when modern changes drive them out, this well-known spirit seems content with his lodgings. He may even choose to stay another hundred years or so.

Captain Harper and the Phantoms of the River

Jeffrey Hull

"The sea never changes and its works,
for all the talk of men, are wrapped in mystery."
Joseph Conrad
1857-1924

Captain Harper and the Phantoms of the River

It was December 24, 1897, and the steamer *Wilmington* was preparing for its evening run downriver to Southport. A freak storm had raged unceasingly, bringing with it stinging sleet, rain, and even flurries of snow. Captain John Harper had braved the elements for three long days. He knew every inch of the Cape Fear River, in fair weather or foul, but this storm was getting the best of him.

There was no question of cancelling the trip. The steamer *Wilmington*, an excursion boat, also carried the daily mail to Southport. Departure from Wilmington was scheduled for 5:00 PM, and a party of holiday revelers loaded with Christmas gifts from their all-day shopping spree hastened on board the ship for the journey home. They were glad to get out of the cold. The brave captain weighed anchor, and the steamer began cutting a careful path through the rough currents. The ship had scarcely gotten underway when the captain heard the voice of his engineer through the speaking tube.

"Captain Harper, sir, there's trouble with the furnace."

"What seems to be the matter?"

"A rivet's broken loose, sir. It's going to take awhile to fix it. Maybe five or six hours."

With that, the captain informed the passengers of the delay, putting a damper on their Christmas cheer. Before long a barge came and towed the steamer to shore and all the passengers, except one, left the ship for more comfortable quarters. The fury of the storm had not subsided; rather it had increased, and the wind swirled the snow around in white funnels mixed with blankets of blinding sleet.

A single passenger remained on board, undaunted by the turn of events and willing to take a chance that the trip to Southport would be made that night. Captain Harper settled back, pipe in hand. Knowing there was nothing he could do, he was ready to enjoy his favorite pastime, storytelling. But it was the stranger who seemed bent on telling the tales, and the captain puffed away contentedly as he listened.

The conversation went back and forth, each man recalling stories of Scotsmen they had known. Since there were many prominent citizens from Scotland who had settled in the Cape Fear area, their stories continued for some time.

One of the stories told by McMillan, for that was the stranger's name, was about his great-grandfather, William McMillan of Edinburgh, who had settled in Robeson County. During the Revolutionary War, William McMillan was charged with treason for his loyalty to the colonies. He was captured by the British and brought to Wilmington, along with two other Highland Whigs, and thrown into jail. Within a short time the three were taken away from the city to stand trial. The trial was a mockery, conducted early in the afternoon, and the men were sentenced to be shot. The place of execution was the site of some old ruins between Orton Plantation and the town of Brunswick.

"Two of the Scotsmen were fired upon and dropped bleeding and dying to the ground." McMillan continued. "But my great-grandfather was a powerful man, a champion with the curling stone. He broke away from his guards, and ran through the sheltering woods with the speed of a wild animal on the chase. He made it back to his home and lived to be an old man. But from that time on, people in the area have told stories of the two phantom Highlanders who stalk the spot and sometimes also row a phantom boat in search of a vessel to take them back to Scotland."

Captain Harper was impressed with the tale. He loved a good ghost story and was frankly puzzled that he had never heard this particular one. As many times as he'd been on the river, he'd never seen anything resembling a ghost, but he knew some spine-tinglers which he told on stormy nights to entertain the passengers. This would make a good story to add to his collection. He sat, puffing on his pipe, and quietly musing on what he had heard.

A call from the mate disturbed his reverie. The repairs had been made, and the ship was ready to depart. Hours had passed, the barometer was still dangerously low, but the mail must go through, so feeling his way along slowly, the captain guided his vessel downriver through the storm.

"In twenty years I've never seen a night such as this," he said to the passenger.

"I was on a blockade runner during the war,"

McMillan replied. "I sailed through many a rough sea, and I'll have to agree with you, Captain, this is by far the most wretched storm I've ever encountered."

The trip became a battle between the treacherous river and the intrepid captain. He and his mate called out to each other, shouting commands through the howling wind, doing everything in their power to keep the vessel from running aground. But finally, the keel scraped a jetty and stuck fast.

The captain swore, something he never did. Instantly embarrassed, he turned to his passenger and apologized, and in so doing he felt a sense of calm return. There was nothing to do but wait for the turn of the tide to float them clear.

The mate, Peter Jorgensen, made his way to the mid-deck under the cover of the upper level. In spite of the storm, he somehow felt the need to be alone. It was Christmas, and his mind was filled with images of past holidays that brought tears to his eyes. He brushed away the tears with his sleeve and, looking up, he was startled to see the figure of a man standing in front of him. The man was dripping wet, his appearance generally disheveled, a most frightening apparition. Peter was petrified. They were on the river in the middle of the night. Where could the man possibly have come from, and why? Peter could see the man's face clearly in the ship's lights, and there was agony in what he saw.

"Who are you?" he cried. "How did you get here?" But there was no answer. He moved forward to touch the man, and in that moment the figure seemed to melt into the air. Peter was alone.

Peter took the stairs two at a time, rushing to tell the captain. He was pale with fright, hardly able to make a sound. "What is it, man?" the captain asked. "Speak up!"

"I've seen a ghost," he replied weakly.

"You must be drunk," Captain Harper said. Turning to McMillan, the captain said, "Have you ever seen a ghost, sir?"

"No, but I don't doubt that your mate has seen one this night. Let's go and search for the ghost and set his mind at ease."

"Come, Peter and take us to the place where you saw the phantom," the captain said, unable still to take the matter seriously.

With that he started for the door, but Peter Jorgensen spoke up. "Captain, if you had seen what I just saw, you'd understand that I would not go back for another look if you gave me the ship this very night. What I saw is vivid in my mind and will not go away. It was most certainly a ghost, how else could it have vanished before my very eyes?"

Not knowing what to make of the strange story, Captain Harper called the crew together and questioned each in turn, but not one had seen anything. With that, the captain began a search of the ship. Nothing was amiss. Captain Harper was disturbed now. He could see that his passenger was also uneasy.

McMillan spoke. "Something ill-favored is about to happen, Captain. I feel it." He told the captain that he thought what Peter had seen had been a warning of some impending danger.

The tide was rising, and the ship suddenly began a

pitching motion that freed it from the obstruction; the rough waves propelled it forward. Surprised by the sudden motion, the men were even more startled by a shrill cry that was heard above the storm. A human cry that seemed to come from the far shore. The sea grew rougher, and to calm the fears of the crew, Captain Harper signaled for a stop. The steamer pitched back and forth in the watery trough. Peter was sure he had heard the sound of a siren, a distress signal. And then the horrifying shriek was heard again. McMillan looked panic-stricken.

"We can't send out help; we'd never make it in these rough seas," the captain said, almost positive that the sounds were coming from the water, not the land. He ordered his crew to stand by. He gave the wheel to McMillan to hold, so that he might go and see for himself what was wrong. Once more the howling cries for help were heard. The captain ordered the ship forward at dead slow.

The storm was beginning to subside, and a few stars were twinkling here and there, giving just enough light to see a vague shoreline. Suddenly an object appeared on the river before them, enveloped in an eerie incandescent light. By now, the captain was convinced that something mysterious and terrifying was happening. The object came toward them, growing larger and glowing with such an intense light that all could see it clearly. It appeared to be the rotting hulk of a barge covered with seaweed and other sea life, foul-smelling and slimy.

Captain Harper rubbed his eyes in disbelief. He turned to McMillan and said, "Your stories seem to have brought the ghosts of the river out tonight. I don't intend to linger here. There's something unnatural taking place."

"There are men in trouble. The cries are human," McMillan answered.

The captain disagreed. "That sound, sir, fills the air from all directions; it does not come from that stinking barge there."

The barge drew nearer and the horrified men on board the *Wilmington* trembled at what they now beheld. Two men, obviously Highlanders, knelt on the grimy deck in kilts that hung in dirty shreds, Their ravaged bodies were battered and bloody. Their hair, matted and filthy, resembled the slimy seaweed that covered the barge. No sound came from their lips, but their faces bore a beseeching look of suffering, and their arms were uplifted in a gesture of supplication. Heavy chains had rubbed their legs raw and bleeding.

The captain was aghast and shouted, "Throw those men a line."

Peter Jorgensen, whose fear by now had reached monumental proportions, nevertheless picked up the heavy line and leaned forward, to fling the rope over. A sudden wave seemed to heave the rotting barge out of the water, almost hurling it at the ship. And in that instant it disappeared. Not a whisper came from anyone on the deck. The men were stunned into silence.

Finally, the captain was able to speak and gave the order to move forward. Within minutes, the air was filled once more with dreadful, penetrating shrieks.

"Captain, look to starboard, sir. It's a shipwreck."

Skillfully the captain turned the ship, narrowly missing the capsized vessel with two half-drowned seaman barely hanging on. Carefully the captain brought his vessel alongside, and the weary, shivering men were hauled on board. Peter moved closer and held up his lantern to look at them. His sudden scream brought the captain immediately to his side.

"It's him, Captain. The ghost I saw earlier on the ship. It's him!" Peter pointed toward one of the sailors.

"But it can't be," Captain Harper said, still registering his shock.

With that McMillan stepped out of the shadows and said knowingly. "It was his spirit, Captain. I've heard of such things happening in times of great distress."

"If you can explain this, sir, then explain the barge we saw."

"That I canna do, Captain," McMillan said, lapsing into his soft Scottish brogue.

The shipwrecked sailors were given food and some warm clothes. At last, they were able to tell how their ship had foundered in the storm. The captain, mate, and three crew members had perished, they said. They could not yet believe their good fortune in being rescued before being drowned or freezing to death in the icy waters.

Upon hearing Peter Jorgensen's strange story, the sailor, whom Peter had recognized from his ghostly encounter earlier that night, told the anxious men that he knew nothing of the incident. He swore he had never seen Peter before, although he did admit he had been delirious for a time and thought he had seen the steamer coming to rescue them.

The horrors of the night began to fade with the coming of a dawn more beautiful than any of the men had ever seen. As the steamer *Wilmington* pulled into its berthing place in Southport, a silent prayer of thanks went up from all on board. It was Christmas, the season of miracles, and each man on board had witnessed one that night.

Adapted from "A Colonial Apparition"
by James Sprunt
(With permission)

The Last Battle

Robert Blanton

"The spirits of the dead who stood
In life before thee are again
In death around thee..."
Edgar Allan Poe
1809-1849

The Last Battle

Sandy dunes rise in silhouette against the evening sky.
Amid the waving sea oats, a single figure, clad in the gray uni-
form of a Confederate general, stands looking out to sea.
Without warning the general lifts his sword, appearing to rally
an unseen regiment against an equally invisible enemy. There is
no sound save the gentle tattoo of the waves against the beach,
and the soft whisper of the wind. Almost as quickly as the fig-
ure appears, it is gone.

It is well known that the phantoms of those who die
a violent death often return to the scene of that violence as if
to right some wrong or to complete some unfinished task.
The great battlefields of the past are a testament to such phenomena. Thousands of visitors claim to have seen the ghosts
of Gettysburg, and thousands more swear they have heard
the echoes of the guns, and the cries of the wounded and
dying on the empty beaches of Normandy. This is the story
of a great general's last battle, and the restless spirit which
seems to watch over the remains of the old sand fort where
the battle took place.

The seaports of the Confederacy had fallen like dominoes under Federal attacks until there was only one left open: the port at Wilmington. General William Whiting was the commanding officer in charge of the defense of Wilmington, a post he had held and managed admirably for many months. In 1862, Whiting, along with four other generals had approved the plans which Colonel Lamb, the newly appointed commandant, had proposed for Fort Fisher. Colonel Lamb had arrived in July of that year and had worked tirelessly along with General Whiting to build the fort into a masterpiece of military engineering. Whiting knew that a major attack on Fort Fisher was inevitable even though its guns had thus far been able to protect the blockade runners from Yankee warships and keep this route open for supplies to the Confederacy.

The long expected attack came on the night of December 23, 1864. General Benjamin Butler with reluctant permission from General Grant had moved the 295 foot *Louisiana*, disguised as a blockade runner, to within a few hundred yards of the shore. The ship was loaded with 215 tons of gunpowder with a timed detonation device. Butler's idea was that the ship would explode and blow up the fort. The explosion lit the sky like a brilliant fireworks display and was just as harmless. Though damage to the fort was minimal, the fiasco caused a great deal of damage to General Butler's reputation.

On the following day, the largest fleet ever assembled under the American flag pounded Fort Fisher with artillery. As fierce as this attack was, it was ineffective against the well-designed earthworks of the fort. On Christmas Day an infantry attack was launched, but Butler, surveying the scene from the deck of a tugboat, ordered the men withdrawn and hastened to leave himself. The attempt to capture the fort was a miserable failure. General Terry was ordered to take Butler's place.

President Lincoln and General Grant were resolved that the supply route through Wilmington must be shut down. Without those supplies, both Lincoln and Grant knew that the Confederacy would fall. Following the unsuccessful assault in December, rumors were flying fast that another, much heavier assault was planned. Grant was determined that this battle would be the last; and so it was.

In the thick of the rumors about the impending naval attack came unexpected orders from the Secretary of War to General Whiting: "Your superior in rank, Gen. Bragg, is charged with the command and defense of Wilmington." General Whiting, though not replaced by Bragg, was now second in command. Colonel Lamb was bitterly disappointed, feeling that "no one was so capable of defending the Cape Fear as the brilliant officer who had given so much of his time and ability for its defense." Whiting took the news bravely and redoubled his efforts to assist Colonel Lamb in preparing for an even greater bombardment by Federal forces. The last battle would soon begin.

On January 12, 1865, a great armada of Union warships reached New Inlet on the Cape Fear coast of North Carolina. The ships began their blistering barrage almost as soon as they reached their destination. Colonel William Lamb knew that Bragg must have sighted the fleet off Masonborough from his position north of the peninsula, yet no word of warning had come from the general. It was to be the "greatest bombardment in history up to that time."

When the naval barrage began, 6000 men from General Robert Hoke's Division of Lee's Army of Northern Virginia were entrenched at "Sugar Loaf," a high sand hill that stood approximately seven miles north of Federal Point, known during the war as Confederate Point. Bragg had made this his headquarters. Despite the repeated telegrams which General Bragg received from both Lamb and Whiting requesting help, he refused to dispatch those troops to assist them in the battle, declaring it to be a lost cause. On the first day of the attack, Whiting realized that Bragg was not going to come to the aid of the besieged troops, so he took a boat downriver and joined Colonel Lamb himself. "I have come to share your fate, my boy," he told the young colonel. "You are to be sacrificed. The last thing I heard Gen. Bragg say, was to point out a line to fall back upon, when Fort Fisher fell."

On the evening of January 13, unopposed enemy troops, numbering about 8,500, had poured ashore and put up entrenchments on either side as they began their approach to the fort. Without help, Whiting knew the fall of Fort Fisher was just a matter of time. The urgent entreaties to General Bragg by telegram were to no avail. His troops had been ordered some sixteen miles away. There were only 1,900 Confederates with 44 guns to defend the fort against ten thousand men and 600 heavy guns afloat. Yet the bloody battle would last for three days and nights. The fury of the battle was unbelievable. Colonel Lamb later referred to it as a "magnificent struggle unsurpassed in ancient or modern warfare."

On the final day of battle, General Whiting saw the

Federal flags being raised. Rallying his troops around him, he charged forward to the traverses which held the gunchambers where the flags were. Hand-to-hand combat ensued. Finally one traverse was recaptured. As he was climbing the other, General Whiting reached for the Federal flag to tear it down. Instead, two bullets felled the general, mortally wounding him. A short while later, Colonel Lamb was also wounded. Even so, the battle continued for many hours before the Union victory was complete. General Whiting was taken prisoner and moved to Fort Columbus on Governor's Island in New York harbor.

From his deathbed, Whiting wrote to General Lee regarding General Bragg: "I demand, in justice to the country, to the army, and to myself, that the course of this officer be investigated....I do not know what he was sent to Wilmington for. I had hoped that I was considered competent; I acquiesced with feelings of great mortification. My proper place was in command of the troops you sent to support the defense; then I should not now be a prisoner, and an effort, at least, would have been made to save the harbor...."

On March 10, 1865, General Whiting died. Less than a month later, on April 9, Lee surrendered at Appomattox.

*   *   *

The war had been over for a number of years when a Civil War reunion was held at Fort Fisher. Three returning veterans outfitted in their fading battle dress had spent the day greeting old friends and reliving some of the memories of that terrible last battle. They talked about the bravery of their beloved General Whiting, remembered fondly as "Little

Billy."

It was late in the afternoon as the men walked along the sandy earthworks of the ruined fort. They thought they saw in the distance a fellow veteran standing atop one of the old gun emplacements. Perhaps it was someone they had not yet spoken with, they thought, and they waved in greeting. There was no response. As they drew nearer, they were struck dumb in shock and disbelief. In the twilight, they recognized the general who had led them in battle. He was waving his sword, seeming to urge his men forward in a show of force against the enemy. Diminutive in stature and dressed in the gray uniform of the South, there was no mistaking the valiant General William Henry Chase Whiting. The men watched in panic-stricken awe, knowing that the scene which now unfolded before their very eyes had actually taken place many years before. As they continued to watch, the figure faded away.

In the years following, others who had worn the uniform of the Confederacy witnessed the same spectral reenactment and wondered at what they saw. Today, there are people who say they, too, have seen the general in the shadows on top of the dunes, sword in hand, leading his final charge.

It was said of General Whiting that "he died as he had lived—the modest Christian gentleman, the lovely man, the brave unflinching soldier." Even death could not deter the courageous general from his duty.

The Grieving Ghost
of Bald Head Island

Robert Blanton

"Did I recollect how the wreckers
Wrecked Theodosia Burr
Off this very shore?"

Robert Frost
1874-1963

The Grieving Ghost of Bald Head Island

On the night of December 30, 1812, a small pilot boat sailed stealthily out of the harbor at Georgetown, South Carolina. Aboard was Theodosia Burr Alston, the beautiful young wife of Joseph Alston, the governor of that state. Among her belongings was a unique oil portrait of herself, painted on mahogany and adorned by a handsome gilt frame. The portrait was a gift for her beloved father, whom she was going to visit in New York.

Theodosia's father was the notorious Aaron Burr, one-time vice-president of the United States, but remembered by history buffs as the victor in a fatal duel with Alexander Hamilton, his political enemy. Following the duel, Burr was arrested and brought to trial for treasonous activities, but the evidence showed that even though he had plotted treason, he had not actually committed the act, and he was therefore acquitted. Feelings ran high against Burr, and he left for France where he lived in poverty for four years. Finally, in 1812, he responded to his only daughter's

113

entreaties to return to America, and he waited anxiously for the ship which would bring her to meet him in New York.

Knowing that sentiment was still fierce against Burr and fearing that Theodosia might be a target of this hatred, Joseph Alston had taken every precaution to make his wife's voyage to New York as discreet and protected as possible. Alston's efforts were in vain. Theodosia, and all on board her ship, disappeared and were never heard from again.

Many years later, two criminals, awaiting execution in Norfolk, Virginia, swore that they had been among a pirate crew that had captured the *Patriot* and said that the crew and passengers were made to walk the plank. Another avowed crew member turned up even later in Michigan. This man claimed to have been haunted for years by the memory of a beautiful young woman who pleaded for her life—a young woman who begged to be allowed to visit her father in New York.

Local tradition strongly suggests that Theodosia's vessel, the *Patriot*, did indeed fall prey to pirates off the coast of Cape Fear, and that the crew had to walk the plank. Some think that Theodosia met the same fate, but others believe that she was taken ashore by the pirates at Smith Island (now Bald Head). Legend has it that she was able to escape from her pirate guards and find refuge among the dunes, until finally, realizing that she had no hope of rescue, she rushed headlong into the sea and drowned. When her two guards were sent to search for her and returned empty-handed, they were hanged. It is said that their wandering spirits may be seen at midnight on the island, searching still for their captive. And the tragic Theodosia...does her spirit also roam the island?

During World War II, two Coast Guardsmen, patrolling the beaches of Bald Head on horseback, were watching for enemy submarines, or saboteurs who might have been sent ashore by such craft. Wary of anything out of the ordinary, one of the men spotted something and alerted the other. "Look there, do you see her?" he whispered. "A woman in a long, flowing dress!" The Coast Guardsmen called to the woman to halt and rode toward her, but both were startled to see her disappear as if into "thin air."

The two men were again on patrol several nights later, and to their surprise and horror, the phantom figure reappeared. When the same command to "Halt!" was ignored, one of the Coast Guardsmen fired his weapon. In utter shock he dropped his gun and turned to his companion to say that the bullet seemed to pass right through the filmy apparition. Again, the vision vanished before their frightened eyes.

The two servicemen were in Southport the following day and became engaged in conversation with an old fisherman from that community. They related the details of their recent unexplained encounters, still unsure whether what they had seen might not have been a spy. The wizened fisherman responded with a story of his own and was quick to tell them that while bullets would do no harm, they also would not help the situation. The fisherman identified the wraith they had seen as the ghost of Theodosia Burr.

He, too, had seen her, he said. It was in the beginning days of the war. Although he had spotted the specter many times in the past, this particular time she seemed to be crying and pointing toward the sea. He had the feeling that the woman was trying to tell him something. Disturbed, but unsure of how to respond, the fisherman did nothing. "The next morning," he continued, "we found a wrecked, burned-out tanker offshore, a victim of an enemy torpedo. If I had only known how to interpret that ghostly warning," he said, "we might have been able to save that tanker." The old fisherman went on to give his opinion that somehow Theodosia Burr was trying to warn her countrymen, maybe in an effort to prove that members of the Burr family were patriots and not traitors.

The stories of the "Theodosia" legend have persisted for almost two hundred years. Reece Swan, who was caretaker on Bald Head for a number of years, said he has heard the stories all his life. He was familiar with the account of the Coast Guardsmen, but could not recall who the men were. "I've seen unexplained lights on the island many times myself," he said, "not gases either, just mysterious lights that had no business being there."

With the rapidly expanding development of Bald Head Island, and the throngs of people who now inhabit the island, it is not likely that Theodosia's lost spirit continues to haunt the shoreline. But, there are those who are convinced she once was there, others who look for her still on dark nights as they stroll along the beach, and some who give no credence at all to the stories of ghosts. The best mysteries, it has been said, are those which remain unsolved.

Oakdale Cemetery

Virginia Wright-Frierson

"Death is the side of life which is turned away from   us."
Rainer Maria Rilke
1875-1926

Oakdale Cemetery

Hidden away in a garden-like setting of azaleas, dog-woods and exquisite natural beauty, Oakdale Cemetery is like no other in the South. Behind the ornate iron gates and fences, there is every type of funereal art...carved mausoleums, angels with outstretched arms, lambs, crosses, flowers... some grand, some simple, but each with a story to tell. Stories of strange burials always seem to evoke a peculiar fascination among devotees of the supernatural, and this historic old cemetery has more than its share. Each evening at five o'clock when the gates are closed and locked, all appears tranquil. The moss-covered monuments stand in silence; the landscape is a visualization of serenity and peace. Yet who knows what restless spirits haunt these hallowed grounds once the city has settled into sleep?

Perchance, the ghosts of some four hundred unknown Confederate soldiers buried in Oakdale stalk the site seeking recognition for their brave deeds, longing for remembrance instead of eternal rest in unmarked graves.

Or perhaps the cemetery hides the ghost of Rose O'Neal Greenhow, known as *Rebel Rose*, heroine and spy for the Confederacy, buried beneath a simple stone cross. Mrs. Greenhow's death was sudden and tragic, the kind which often occasions subsequent hauntings. She was returning from England aboard the *Condor* with $2,000 in gold earned from the publication of a book dealing with her experiences. Presumably the gold was for the Confederacy. Trying to enter New Inlet in a storm, her ship met the waiting guns of the *USS Niphon*. In the ensuing chase, the *Condor* ran aground. Not long before, Mrs. Greenhow had spent time in a Yankee prison. Fear of recapture by Union forces caused her to risk her life in a small dinghy. The captain begged her to stay with the ship, but she was adamant about leaving. Almost as soon as it was lowered into the mountainous waves, the tiny craft overturned. Rose Greenhow's body washed ashore on Ft. Fisher and was brought to Wilmington to be laid out for burial. It was said that she was beautiful, even in death. In tribute to her loyalty to the Confederate cause, her body was wrapped in a Confederate flag, and at her burial she was given full military honors. Hundreds attended and mourned her.

There are conflicting reports about the disposition of the gold she was carrying for the Confederacy. Some said the gold was sewn into her clothing. Others insisted it was secured in a pouch and hung from a chain around her neck. But all believed that the weight of the gold was responsible for her drowning.

Could it be that she searches for it still?

Even the story of the establishment of the cemetery and the first burial there has its own tragic twist. The city of Wilmington was ravaged by epidemics in the early to mid 1800s: yellow fever, diphtheria, typhoid and more took their toll on the population. It became apparent that the small, local churchyard cemeteries were no longer adequate. In 1852, a committee was appointed to look into the matter of a new cemetery. Sixty-five acres on the east side of Burnt Mill Creek were chosen and on April 8, 1854, the purchase was completed for a sum of $1,100. Dr. Armand J. de Rosset, a prominent physician, had the honor of being elected to serve as the first president of the Board of Directors of Oakdale Cemetery. Ironically, the first interment in the new cemetery turned out to be Dr. deRosset's own daughter, just six years old. It is said that following her death the good doctor gave up his medical practice, unable to accept the fact that all his years of experience and medical expertise were not enough to save his own precious child. Surely, the most poignant epitaph in the entire cemetery is the one that marks her grave. Beneath the carved figure of a tiny lamb are the words, "Our Little Annie."

Dr. deRosset would not be the only grief-stricken father to bring his daughter's remains to rest in Oakdale. A few years later, Captain Silas Martin, a well-to-do Wilmington merchant, would do the same, after a bizarre set of circumstances.

For as long as he could remember, Captain Martin had dreamed of taking his children with him on a voyage to foreign lands. One thing after another prevented him. Yet the day he had dreamed of finally arrived in the spring of 1857. Why his wife chose to stay behind is not known. Perhaps she had household responsibilities she could not leave. Notwithstanding, Captain Martin set sail with two of his older children: Nancy, twenty-four, and John Salter, thirty-four.

Soon after their departure, Nancy fell ill. Far from port, with no physician on board, and only limited medical supplies available, there was little that could be done for her, and the young woman's condition grew worse. The captain was finally able to make port in Cardenas, Cuba, but it was too late to save his daughter. Nancy Martin died shortly after the ship docked. The tormented father could not bear to bury his daughter among strangers on foreign soil, neither could he stand the thought of burying her at sea. So he had her body secured in a chair, then lowered into a large cask filled with whiskey and rum for a preservative, and sealed. Bound by business commitments, Captain Silas Martin decided to continue his lengthy voyage. The decision was a fateful one. Several months later, at the height of a sudden storm, his son, John Salter, disappeared from the ship and was presumed to have been washed overboard and drowned. His body was never recovered.

With the second tragedy, the ship turned back. Upon his return, Captain Martin had to break the news of the terrible misfortune to his wife. The distraught parents determined it would be unwise after so long a time to transfer their daughter's remains to a coffin. Instead, Nancy Martin was buried in the cask of liquor. The marker over her grave bears only her pet name, "Nance." On the family monument nearby is engraved her full name and the date of her death as well as the name of Nancy Martin's brother and the somber words, "Lost at Sea, September, 1857."

Heroes and children are not the only spirits that might manifest themselves in this timeless old burial ground. If animals can "come back," old Boss may be there still, guarding the grave of William A Ellerbrook, a riverboat captain, who lost his life in 1880 while fighting a raging downtown fire. According to witnesses, Ellerbrook's dog, Boss, rushed fearlessly into the flames and tried to save his master.

Both perished. When the two were found, Captain Ellerbrook was lying face down trapped by a fallen timber. Trying to pull his master to safety, the dauntless animal was overcome by smoke. A torn piece of Ellerbrook's coat was found clamped tightly in his jaws. The dog had sacrificed his own life in an attempt to save his master. It seemed fitting that the two, united in death, should be laid to rest in the same coffin, and so they were. On Captain Ellerbrook's monument there is the sculpted image of a dog and the words, "Faithful Unto Death."

In 1856, a senseless death took place resulting from what is thought to be the last political duel fought in the South. Dr. W. C. Willkings was a well-respected young physician, who was also a popular politician. He was advised of a publication written by his erstwhile friend, Joseph H. Flanner, alleging that certain statements made by Dr. Willkings in a political speech were false. Angered by the charges, Willkings challenged Flanner to a duel. Willkings was killed, and Flanner was held blameless because he had been forced to take action to defend himself. A towering marker was erected to Dr. Willkings' memory by his political friends, although his name was misspelled "Wilkings" on the monument. Some say that the ghost of Willkings still walks—haunting not the cemetery but the spot in downtown Wilmington where he spent his last night.

For almost one hundred fifty years, funeral processions have made their way along the winding lanes in Oakdale Cemetery. Families have mourned their loved ones in the satisfying certainty that the spirits of the dead have found a sweet release. Have these spirits indeed gone on to immortality, or are there some which continue to exist on another plane, outside the physical body, until their business here on earth is complete? One can only wonder.

"The South has her share of ghosts.
Souls so full of life take their time in departing -
some hover for only a few minutes or days,
some stalk and haunt for eternity."

from *Keeper of the Moon*
by Tim McLaurin

Historical Notes

HISTORICAL NOTES

Samuel Jocelyn

The story of Samuel Jocelyn was first told in public by Colonel James G. Burr in a lecture given February 3, 1890, on the stage of the old Wilmington Opera House (now The Thalian Hall Center for the Performing Arts). The text for part of the lecture, that which told of the disinterment, was written for Colonel Burr by one of Wilmington's most respected matrons, Mrs. Catherine Kennedy. The story she wrote was an eyewitness account given to her by none other than Louis Toomer, the friend who had assisted Alexander Hostler in the exhumation of the body. A member of one of Wilmington's wealthiest and most prominent families, the deRossets, Mrs. Kennedy was married to Dr. William Kennedy, pastor of the Front Street Methodist Church. Few, if any, would have doubted the words of Mrs. Kennedy, who was known to all in the community for her philanthropic work and dedication to public service.

Further proof of the veracity of the strange tale told that night was the testimony of Colonel James G. Burr, a Wilmington native, highly esteemed by all who knew him. A biographical sketch of Colonel Burr by James Sprunt in *Chronicles of the Cape Fear River* has this to say. "He was much interested in local history and was regarded as an authority...." Sprunt paints a picture of a man who loved the "tales and traditions of the Cape Fear." Colonel Burr stated that he had learned the facts from his mother, a close relative of Alexander Hostler. Hostler himself had given the bizarre details of the story to Mrs. Burr. Perhaps it was the indisputable credibility of these two contemporaries that convinced all who heard the strange tale that it was most certainly a true story.

Thalian Hall

Designed by the foremost theatre architect of the nineteenth century, John Montague Trimble, Thalian Hall was completed in 1858, and today is the only Trimble-designed theatre still surviving. The theatre's elegant "floating balconies" are a hallmark of its architectural excellence, and its acoustical qualities remain unsurpassed. Known formerly as The Wilmington Opera House, the theatre is a part of a larger building that houses the City Hall and at one time also included the local library.

When John T. Ford, builder of Ford's Theatre in Washington, D.C., took over the management of Thalian Hall in 1869, the theatre became part of a touring circuit of Ford's theatres that eventually brought most of the famous actors of that day to the Wilmington stage.

For almost a century and a half, Shakespearean drama, musical comedy, minstrel shows, classical concerts, eloquent oratory, and more have delighted Thalian Hall audiences. Joseph Jefferson, Maurice Barrymore, Oscar Wilde, Agnes Morehead, Lillian Russell, Marian Anderson, John Phillips Sousa, and even Buffalo Bill are among the eminent entertainers who have performed there. But the moments of unforgettable splendor have been coupled with periods of waning interest and neglect, even abuse. During World War II, wrestling and prize fights were the main attraction. Later, the quality of the performances improved, but funding soon put the future of the theatre in doubt.

Through it all, various civic groups, the arts community, and private individuals kept alive the dream of preserving one of Wilmington's most valuable architectural treasures. That dream became a reality in 1990 after a multimillion dollar renovation. The facade and lobby have a contemporary, "uptown" look, but the interior of the main theatre retains its traditional red, green, and gold color scheme, richly adorned with gilt. An expansion added a studio theatre, a new entrance, and updated council chambers for the City Hall portion of the building. It reopened as the Thalian Hall Center for the Performing Arts.

Though an account in the *Wilmington Daily Herald* in 1859 called the building "grand and imposing," actor Tyrone Power probably captured the essence of the theatre's enduring appeal best. He wrote after a visit in 1958, Thalian Hall "has an atmosphere and a history shared by all too few remaining theatres of its kind in this country."

Captain John W. Harper

Perhaps no seafaring man was ever more loved or respected than Captain John W. Harper. He was born in New Hanover County, November 28, 1856. At sixteen, he went to sea, working first as a deck hand. By age nineteen, he had become a licensed master. For almost forty years Captain Harper plied the Cape Fear River with his ships, the most famous of which was the steamer *Wilmington*. During that time he gained a reputation not only as a successful sea captain, but also as a teller of tales. Captain Harper's fame as a storyteller grew to such proportions that he earned the nickname "The Mark Twain of the Cape Fear River."

Dr. James Sprunt wrote of him in his book, *Tales and Traditions of the Lower Cape Fear*, published in 1896 and dedicated to Capt. Harper. "As we approach the gangway of this stately steamer...we are promptly met by the Commander and owner, a dignified stalwart specimen of the American sailor and gentleman....His name is John W. Harper, and he is said to be the favorite skipper of North Carolina."

An editorial in the *Wilmington Star News* on September 18, 1917, noted "Sorrow, therefore, will be widespread because Captain Harper has passed from this world and has closed a life of great usefulness to the people of this city and Southport...His name is blessed among thousands, and we cannot recall the death of a man who will be more universally mourned."

General William H. C. Whiting
"Little Billy"

General Whiting was born in Mississippi. He graduated first in his class from West Point . An account in Dr. James Sprunt's *Chronicles of the Cape Fear River* notes that "His wife was a Miss Walker of Wilmington, and at the outbreak of the war he was a Wilmingtonian by adoption, well-known and highly esteemed." For a brief period after the fall of Ft. Sumter he assumed command in Wilmington, but was shortly thereafter called as chief engineer for General Joseph E. Johnston in Virginia. In 1862, he was again placed in command of Wilmington's defenses.

Before the war, General Whiting had worked with the Corps of Engineers on a project to improve the harbor and the lower part of the Cape Fear River. His knowledge of the topography and his experience were very helpful to him in planning defense strategy for Wilmington and Fort Fisher. His headquarters during the war were in the old deRosset house that stood on the northwest corner of Third and Market Streets. It was from there that Whiting left to go to Fort Fisher.

Although General Whiting died a prisoner in the hospital at Fort Columbus on Governor's Island in New York Harbor, he was given the esteem he deserved at his funeral. An article on March 13, 1865, in the *New York Daily News* reported: "A very large concourse of people was present, and the profoundest respect was paid to the deceased, and his sorrowing relatives and friends." There was a lengthy description of the funeral in the article.

His obituary in a North Carolina paper had this to say: "The death of Major General Whiting deserves more than a passing notice...But it was not in the field only, that General Whiting's abilities were displayed. Assigned to the command of the defenses of the Cape Fear, he exhibited...a genius and skill as an engineer which won the unstinted praise of every military judge—praise that was even accorded by the enemy."

No leader was ever more loved than "Little Billy." He was only 5 feet 2 inches tall, but he was a giant in the eyes of his men. As Major Sloan, his Chief of Ordnance said, they "almost worshiped him!"

General Whiting was buried in a New York cemetery, but the body was later exhumed and finally laid to rest in Oakdale Cemetery. His sword and uniform are part of the Civil War collection at the Cape Fear Museum.

The Portrait of Theodosia Burr Alston

The portrait which Theodosia Burr Alston was believed to have with her on her fateful voyage is a story in itself. Though Theodosia never reached her destination in New York, by an amazing intervention of fate, the portrait found its way to the home of a descendent of the Burr family in that very city more than a century later.

For more than fifty years, the portrait seemed lost. Then in the year 1869, Dr. W. G. Poole, from Elizabeth City, was spending his vacation on the Outer Banks when he received an emergency call to treat an elderly woman who lived a short distance from Nags Head. The woman, a Mrs. Mann, had never been treated by a physician, and she was understandably frightened as well as skeptical. When her treatment proved successful, she was extremely grateful to the doctor and wanted to pay him. Although Dr. Poole had returned several times to check on her, accompanied by his small daughter, he knew the old woman's meager circumstances and refused to accept any money. Mrs. Mann was a proud woman and insisted that he take something in return for his services. She offered him an unusual and very lovely portrait hanging in her parlor, which he and his young daughter had admired.

The doctor was delighted but curious as to how such a fine portrait came to hang in such a modest home. Mrs. Mann told him that years before, in January of 1813, her first husband, a Mr. Tillett, and some of his friends had salvaged the painting and an assortment of other articles from an abandoned vessel that had drifted aground near Nags

Courtesy of The Lewis Walpole Library, Yale University

Head. When the men went on board, they found the table set as if for breakfast. Trunks had been broken open and several vases, some silk dresses, and the oil portrait were lying scattered about. The condition of the boat, the fact that its rudder had been tied and it had been set adrift, strongly suggested to these men of the sea that pirates had looted the valuables and forced the passengers and crew overboard.

Dr. Poole returned to his home in Elizabeth City with his prized possession. In the course of time, Dr. Poole chanced upon some evidence which led him to believe that the portrait was that of Theodosia Burr. He contacted members of the Burr family and sent photographs of the portrait. The resemblance was too strong to deny, and the family was convinced that it was truly the lost Theodosia. Some of the family even made a trip to the doctor's home in North Carolina to see the painting.

Years passed, and nothing more was heard of it until one day, according to a report in an old newspaper, an art aficionado in Brooklyn, New York, read a book by Charles Burr Todd, entitled *The True Aaron Burr*, in which reference was made to the portrait. Enough details of the theories regarding Theodosia's death and the oil painting were mentioned to pique the gentleman's curiosity. His name was Herbert Pratt. Pratt contacted a local art dealer, a Mr. MacBeth, who immediately set about to locate the artwork and purchase it for him. It was nothing short of incredible that MacBeth was able to do so. Dr. Poole had been dead for years, but in 1913, the art dealer traced the portrait to Anna Poole Overman, Dr. Poole's daughter, also of Elizabeth City, who was finally persuaded to sell it.

The learned eye of Mr. MacBeth quickly determined

the art treasure to be an authentic representative of the American school of art popular between 1800 and 1810. The portrait perfectly matched early descriptions of Theodosia Burr. In fact, it bore an uncanny resemblance to one of her father painted by John Vanderlyn in 1809. Vanderlyn was the same artist believed to have painted the aristocratic Theodosia. MacBeth purchased the portrait for the Pratt family, but it hung for a time in the MacBeth Art Galleries in New York.

In 1936, MacBeth again arranged a sale, this time to Miss Annie Burr Jennings. After almost 125 years, and an astounding journey, Theodosia's gift had finally reached the home of a family member. Miss Jennings died in 1939 leaving it to her niece, Annie Burr Auchincloss Lewis, of Farmington, Connecticut. Some years later, upon the deaths of Mrs. Lewis and her husband, their estate with all its art treasures was left to Yale University. Theodosia's likeness may be seen to this day in the Lewis home now known as the Lewis-Walpole Library of Yale University.

About the Artwork

Wilmington, North Carolina, has long been known for the richness of its visual arts. The illustrations in this book were drawn by eight area artists who represent a wide range of styles and talent. Several are seasoned veterans already nationally known for their work; others are just beginning their careers. They are listed in alphabetical order.

Robert Blanton is a Wilmington native who attended New Hanover High School. This is his first published artwork.

Davis Canady is a commercial artist with a special interest in cartoons. He owns an independent graphics company, holds a position as a graphic artist for Wordwright Publishing, and teaches ballroom dancing.

Ruth Gratch studied art in New York City but did not become a full-time artist until after a retirement move to Wilmington. Her work appears in several area galleries and in many private collections.

Jeffrey Hull received an undergraduate degree in creative arts from UNC-Charlotte and an MFA from the University of Georgia, and went on to teach at both schools. He has exhibited widely in the Southeast and in New York, and his paintings hang in collections all over the country.

Joan Kaiser does most of her work in oils, primarily portraits, animals, and landscapes. Her work has won several local awards. She is a project coordinator for the Coastal Rehabilitation Hospital at New Hanover Regional Medical Center.

Elizabeth Picklesimer grew up in Morganton and moved to Wilmington in 1994. She studied design at Western Piedmont Community College and currently works in the occupational therapy department at New Hanover Regional Medical Center. In addition to her illustrations inside this book, her work appears on the cover.

Dan Welborn is an Indiana native who moved to the Cape Fear Coast in 1980 after retiring from the Air Force. He began drawing after age fifty, and currently exhibits his work at the City Market in Wilmington.

Virginia Wright-Frierson is known both as a fine artist and an illustrator of children's books. Her paintings have been shown widely all over the United States. She has illustrated six children's books and is the writer/ illustrator of a seventh.

A native North Carolinian, Brooks Newton Preik was
born in Southport and grew up there. She graduated from
St. Mary's Junior College in Raleigh in 1958 and from the
University of North Carolina at Chapel Hill in 1960 with a
degree in Elementary Education. She taught in the public
schools of Virginia, Massachusetts, and North Carolina for
ten years. In 1975, she received her North Carolina Real
Estate Broker's License and is currently in charge of
Advertising and Relocation at Adam & Hilliard Realty.

In 1993, she co-authored a guidebook to the area,
What Locals Know About Wilmington and Its Beaches. She
has published articles in *Encore, Wilmington Coast Magazine,
Wilmington Magazine,* and *Carolina Style.*

In 1995, she won first prize in the Lower Cape Fear
Historical Society's Short Fiction Contest for her short story,
"Kate."

She lives with her husband, Al Preik, in Wilmington.